Preface

1. Next Level Schools

The escalator image on the cover is a reference to movement to the next level as a result of a bias to action. The escalator suggests a new place ahead, a climb to that higher level.

While change and progression in schools can come at a cost and may not be smooth or steady, we are at our best when we can see the evidence of growth and progress. We can delight in looking back and noting the positive differences in culture, performance or processes.

There are a number of well researched instruments, based on performance progressions, that indicate movement to a new level. The National School Improvement Tool is an example of one of these instruments. These types of measurement tools are ideal directional guides supporting the next level analogy promoted in this book.

2. A bias to action

The book's subtitle 'a bias to action' is relevant in every Episode. The term is applied to those behaviours that favour action over inaction. When a leader demonstrates a bias to action their behaviours are consistent, considered and collaborative. They respect the school's context, the people involved and the evidence before them.

In this way persons with a bias to action demonstrate leadership of the community. They keep people together and positively inclined to the changes even while questioning themselves and others about the current state, perhaps even making some uncomfortable in the process. These leaders can hold big dreams or be bold in their outlook. They most likely want steady progress, understanding that overcoming challenges takes planning, persistence and time.

Therefore, the term as applied, and the book itself, does not support impulsive leadership, risky behaviours or maverick leaders.

This book can support your bias to action at the personal and organisational level. Examples of possible scenarios where you will find the Episodes helpful include:

- You are a newly appointed principal, or appointed to a different school as principal
- Similarly, you find yourself in a leadership role where you have additional responsibilities
- You are looking for a fresh approach to your leadership
- You are finding the school's agenda needs renewing and revitalising
- You are a member of an established team or you have commenced work with a new team
- Relationships and culture are limiting the school's potential
- Academic performance is requiring a stronger focus
- You are supervising a group of schools and are seeking to understand the reasons behind particular cultural and educational characteristics

Acknowledgements

Thank you to those who have encouraged me to publish this thinking on school life. My wife, Shelley for her patience and support throughout the writing of this book and my mother Marie. Both exert a huge influence over my thinking, gently correcting my mistakes and showing me better ways to view situations.

Sincere thanks to the many people who have modelled for me the best of leadership. They have helped me understand the transforming possibilities that inspiring and ethical leadership can have on the organisation. These people include many individual teachers, teacher leaders, principals and system supervisors.

In the preparation of this book I would like to acknowledge colleagues Michael Bezzina, Doug Ashleigh, Bronwyn Coe, Joanna Ware and Tony O'Shea for providing proofing, editorial advice and encouragement. Any mistakes are mine alone. Any credits belong to these and other unnamed people who have journeyed with me, helped shape my thinking and challenged me to do better.

I thank former Directors of Education, Rick Johnston (Armidale Catholic Schools) and Pam Betts (Brisbane Catholic Education) for their confidence in me and the many system colleagues I have worked with over the years.

I remain grateful for the professional support of Joanna Ware and Bronwyn Coe who as Executive Assistants worked closely with me in my different roles in the last fifteen years.

Special thanks to Clare Locke (clocke.com.au) for the design elements in this publication.

About the author

Paul Thornton is an education consultant. He retired from full time work in 2021 after 43 years working in a variety of roles in Catholic Education in Queensland and New South Wales. Paul has been a teacher, Assistant Principal, Principal of three schools, a University College Master, education consultant, Assistant Director and Director in urban, regional and rural settings. He retired from Brisbane Catholic Education as Head of School Progress and Performance.

After graduating in 1978 Paul has studied extensively over the years including a PhD from the University of New England (1996) on the Psychological, Physiological and Work Stress of Principals. His educational interests include school leadership, creating collaborative teams, better student outcomes and the wellbeing of staff.

Disclaimer

The material in this publication is of the nature of general comment and does not represent professional advice. It is not intended to be specific guidance for specific circumstances and should not be relied on as the basis for any decision to take action, or not to take action, on any matter canvassed. Readers should always obtain professional and system authority advice as appropriate before they decide on how to use material presented in this publication. To the maximum extent permitted under the law, the author and publisher disclaim all responsibility and liability, to any person, that arises directly or indirectly because the person has taken or not taken action based on the information in this publication.

Copyright © Paul Thornton 2023

No part of this work may otherwise be reproduced or copied in any form without the written permission of Paul Thornton.

ISBN 978-0-6458843-0-2

Contents

Preface — 1

Introduction — 4

Individual leader focus summary map — 6

EPISODE 1 7
A working life in context

EPISODE 2 11
How do I build my capacity?

EPISODE 3 14
Understanding my motivation

EPISODE 4 18
Conducting a professional conversation

EPISODE 5 22
Marks of a teacher leader

EPISODE 6 27
Managing expectations

School team focus summary map — 32

EPISODE 7 33
Next level team

EPISODE 8 38
Using data effectively

EPISODE 9 42
Strong leadership teams and the underlying vision

EPISODE 10 46
Hope is a strategy

EPISODE 11 51
Getting started

EPISODE 12 55
Changing things

EPISODE 13 60
My contribution

School community focus summary map — 64

EPISODE 14 65
Sunnyside schools vs Darkside schools

EPISODE 15 70
Understanding the school around me

EPISODE 16 73
The enrolment challenge

EPISODE 17 77
Maintaining a high performance learning culture

EPISODE 18 81
Moving from planning to collaboration

EPISODE 19 85
Conversations and questions

EPISODE 20 90
Beyond planning

EPISODE 21 94
Everyone has bad days

EPISODE 22 97
Eyes on

EPISODE 23 101
High impact classrooms

EPISODE 24 105
The learning culture

References — 108

Notes — 111

Introduction

NEXT LEVEL SCHOOLS is a practical resource about improvement for the individual leader, school teams and the school community as a whole. Each of the 24 Episodes explores one of these three focus areas using a graphic as an explanatory tool and then drawing on contemporary literature to explain and further explore the concept.

If you are a professional with a bias to action, these resources offer the opportunity to get the learning conversations started.

Why is this important?

There is no doubt key educational and school leadership talking points such as quality teaching, learning growth, school improvement, better student outcomes, evidence based practices and school performance remain hotly debated in society.

The answer to the long standing question, 'What is it to be a good school (or a good leader)?', continues to confound. The media wants easy answers like a return to phonics or evidence based pay for teachers but the lived reality for those in schools is not quite so simple.

The talking points (or issues) surface regularly in the national media, usually in the negative comparative sense and generally painting the progress of Australian education, its teachers and leadership (as measured by NAPLAN and PISA) in a poor light.

Within system organisations and schools, performance issues are a constant focus and subject to much scrutiny. While the level of public commentary around school performance rises and falls according to when and where the media wish to focus, within educational circles these issues are always in focus.

It is important for school leaders to be able to coherently and confidently explain the issues and how they impact the school and even more importantly, what the school is doing to ensure success for students.

Who this book is for

NEXT LEVEL SCHOOLS is centred on the improvement agenda for the individual leader, the different teams within the school and the community as a whole. A range of people in schools will find this resource useful.

This resource is best used as a conversational tool. It is only in the public expression of our values, attitudes and beliefs that we come to fully know ourselves. Listening to others, debating points and reflecting on a position all serve to mould and sharpen our thinking. Knowing stuff in your head is all well and good, but an inability to express it coherently and confidently will convince no one.

This is not an academic text in the traditional sense. The 24 Episodes in this publication are focused on and around the educational theory that drives the performance themes listed above. The Episodes are intended to be professional learning activities that will build individual knowledge, develop team collaboration and promote organisational growth.

Understanding ourselves and others, building individual and group skills and creating a collaborative community are at the heart of any improving organisation. There is no chance of improvement outside of a collaborative community. Teacher quality, school improvement and better student outcomes are indeed worthy, pertinent topics to explore in this environment.

The Episodes take a broad view of leadership, quality and improvement. Leadership is a task for everyone. In this publication it is not solely tied to the one person known as the principal.

Various teams within the school will find the resource useful. This includes formal teams like a leadership team or a school constituted, specialist team such as a pedagogy or wellbeing team.

A narrow focus on only academic results as a measure of quality, as important as this is, or solely on NAPLAN 'Like Student' comparisons, fails to recognise the full social purposes of schooling and the education of the whole child. A balance is required here.

Social/emotional learning, student wellbeing, cultural pursuits, civic education and in many situations, faith and religious purposes, are all important quality markers as well as academic comparisons.

Like many great challenges this is a serious business and the work is never fully completed. It is always a work in progress.

How is the resource presented

The format of the publication is intended to promote thinking and dialogue. Each Episode is structured similarly. The various Episodes are grouped into three focus categories: (i) Individual leader consideration (ii) team exercises and (iii) a school community focus with exercises which are well suited for a whole staff conversation. The three level grouping is intended as a guide and any Episode could be successfully completed in any of the three suggested settings.

A conceptual map or graphic representation commences each Episode and provides the reader with a connecting visual which can be adjusted to suit the individual circumstance. Graphics and visual representations assist with understanding. The associated text draws on the literature, providing the reader with recognised academic thinking and commentary. Good conversation includes a proper recognition of the academic and research dimension, the science behind our work.

Individual and group questions in each Episode can further support the conversation. Engaging as a learner will ensure everyone involved is included. Attending to this work as an 'expert' or being convinced that as a 'principal' you know more will not assist in genuine professional conversation.

The process methodology for each Episode will vary depending on the audience and the situation.

Because the themes are linked, likewise with the Episodes. The reader will find some commonality between certain Episodes with each one taking a slightly different approach. Each of the three focus areas has a summary page showing the complementary relationship between the Episodes within that area.

How to use NEXT LEVEL SCHOOLS

There is no set order to the Episodes and the publication can be commenced at any point enabling the school's most critical issues to be explored first if needed.

To make the most of the resource, first explore the contents relating to the individual leader and then with the team Episodes before launching into any whole staff exercise. There are plenty of team based Episodes that will provide the foundation for good conversation and thinking. Your response and reaction to the individual leader Episodes can be shared with the team. This will further deepen the trust with those close to you.

The graphic representations that start each Episode can be used 'as is' or adjusted as required to suit the school circumstance. These visual representations come in different forms and with the individual reflection and staff conversation pieces at the end of each Episode are intended to promote good conversation. In some of the graphics pages a response space is available and in others the design simply puts the concept in visual form. You are encouraged to consider the challenge of One Step Further at the end of each episode.

There is much wisdom to be shared in schools and each Episode is intended to get people talking about the right things at the right time.

Individual leader focus summary map

E1 A working life in context

The best way to understand personal wellbeing is in a whole-of-life context and not just in an examination of how stressful work (in our case, teaching) might be.

E2 How do I build my capacity

Two significant questions for any teacher should be:

- How do I improve? And
- How do I know I am improving?

E3 Understanding my motivation

If you are engaging with this material chances are you have been around education for some time and have seen enough of good and poor leadership to reflect meaningfully on your own performance and motivations.

E4 Conducting a professional conversation

One of the most basic occurrences in any school situation is the professional conversation with a colleague. This Episode is concerned with those conversations where a concern is raised.

E5 Marks of a teacher leader

Improving teacher quality is a focus in all education systems because it is the pathway to student success, better educational outcomes for the school and stronger student and staff wellbeing.

E6 Managing expectations

As a principal, the management of community expectations is vital.

These Episodes are intended for the individual to complete however they are easily adapted to a small group setting.

The arrows indicate a complementary relationship between Episodes in this focus area.

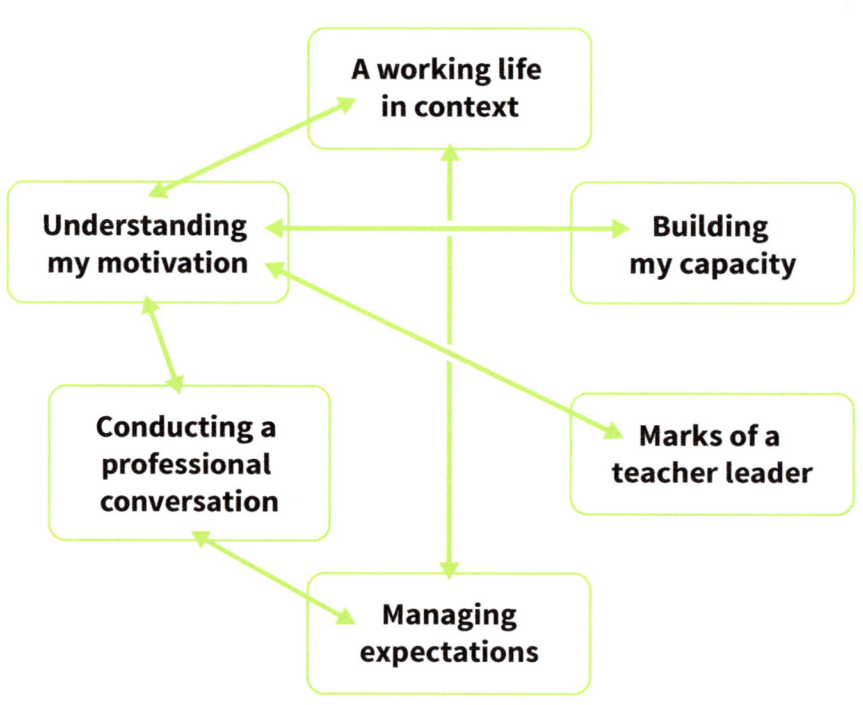

EPISODE 1

A working life in context

TITLE

A working life in context

FOCUS

 Individual Leader

 Leadership Team

 School community

WHY READ THIS

Schools can be stressful places impacting on our wellbeing. If on occasion you feel you do not have the resources to cope with the demands of work or home this Episode might assist you understand the issues.

Psychological Perspective

- Personality and temperament
- Sleep patterns
- Memory and concentration
- Practiced avoidance behaviours
- Level of motivation
- Reaction to change events
- Sense of humour and fun
- Character, ethics and morality

Lifestyle/Workstyle Perspective

- Support groups available
- Friends outside work
- Work taken home after hours
- Employer expectations and demands
- Level of work responsibility
- Qualifications and study needs
- Job advancement concerns
- Job security concerns
- Hours worked per day/week
- Relations within the organisation
- Working conditions
- Relaxation techniques used
- Marital status and relationships
- Family demands
- Hobbies away from work
- Spiritual and meditative resources

Physiological Perspective

- Family medical history
- Diet
- Blood pressure
- Personal fitness regime
- Weight to height ratio
- Medication prescribed
- Use of legal social drugs
- General health
- Resistance to infection
- Immunisation record

Additional considerations: Schools

- Class (or school size)
- Diversity of learners in the class (or school)
- Numbers of complex children and parents
- Level of parental involvement and support
- Demands of committee work (after hours)
- Expertise and engagement of the staff
- System demands
- Numbers of supervisions and duties expected
- Level of resources in the school
- Availability of support staff for teachers
- The school culture
- State of classrooms and the facilities in classes
- Requisite planning, marking, assessing and reporting required

A working life in context

The best way to understand personal wellbeing is in a whole-of-life context and not just in an examination of how stressful work (in our case, teaching) might be.

Perlin (1989) suggests that stress does not spring from a vacuum but can be typically traced back to the person's surrounding social structures and people's place within them. While it's a quote from the 1980's and uses the term 'stress' it reminds us that it is very hard to live life in isolated and separated parts. While wellbeing and stress are related they are not direct substitutes. The intention in this Episode is not to be too academic over the differences but to highlight the ways our wellbeing and our work life are linked.

These days we more commonly refer to wellbeing, and understanding the place of life's structures in our wellbeing remains important. When looking at a person's overall wellbeing any practical model should account for the broader context of the person's life. This certainly includes work but importantly other aspects to life such as family, personality, our physical health and the support structures available to us. These must also be considered.

Wellbeing is a popular topic for all age levels. As wellbeing is part of the human condition everyone has an opinion because we live it every day. And yet, the experience of wellbeing is never quite the same for two people, even when sharing similar jobs or encounters.

The model presented attempts to respond to the challenge of understanding wellbeing in both a holistic and an individualistic manner. Built into this model are distinctive markers to guide the single person. At the same time the model can be applied at the organisational level for groups of people. As well as pointing out problems or potential wellbeing issues, a useful model needs to suggest a course of action for the person or the organisation.

The three wellbeing perspectives of the model; (i) the psychological perspective, (ii) the lifestyle/workstyle perspective and (iii) the physiological perspective are not totally separate entities. They are deliberately intertwined in the daily rhythm of life. Any thorough examination of a person's declining wellbeing needs to consider all three perspectives and not just a single line of response through a single fix (as examples: attend to relaxation, less student numbers in class or find more enjoyment in the day).

For example, a commonly heard remedy for improving wellbeing is to exercise more. That remedy might well be pertinent for an individual who does not exercise at a sufficient level anyway but what about a person who does exercise well or who can't exercise for medical reasons. In any case, in a holistic sense exercise is probably only part of the response.

> Common human traits such as humour, temper and even sleep patterns all affect our general wellbeing.

The three perspectives explained

The centrepiece of the model is the psychological perspective. It is the psychological perspective, our inner life, that is the great mediator as it acts as a type of conductor or insulator of stressful events, effectively supporting our wellbeing or creating the conditions where the pressures of other perspectives outweigh our personal resources to effectively respond, thereby impacting our wellbeing. Personality traits such as our sense of humour, our response to disappointment and our sleep patterns all affect our general wellbeing. The key to the psychological perspective is understanding ourselves and in the case of a working life, the way we respond to the pressures of the job.

Within the psychological perspective there are significant wellbeing markers. This is a lifetime experience, for understanding ourselves better is a never completed job. The reality is that while we prefer to see ourselves as full of good humour, easy with change, highly motivated and acting ethically at all times, we are often not, or at least others do not see us quite like that all the time. The real challenge here is to understand ourselves and our motivations better and where required, adapt and change.

The lifestyle/workstyle perspective effectively takes up all our waking hours and is deliberately joined. Our work and home lives (and the social structures with them) are notoriously difficult to separate. While it might be possible to separate them out in theory, they are simply too linked to cleave apart. Work can be a place of great satisfaction. Just as within the family, it is where we develop as a person and define ourselves. Our work life is where we encounter people, express our opinions, get challenged, grow and change. A work life includes the conditions of work, the climate, the status and the level of responsibility we hold. In a similar manner a home life offers much the same but in different ways. Our family relationships, relaxation, marital status, hobbies and all the resources available to us define us as well. Home is also where we develop, grow and change.

There are some additional considerations in this perspective to take into account the particular circumstances of school life. These are unavoidable if you are going to teach for you will always have students, their parents, other teachers about and work demands to be met.

The third perspective, our physiology, is important in the wellbeing equation. Our body systems and general health are hugely important in wellbeing. Declining wellbeing at work will have its inevitable impact on our health. Declining health will have its inevitable impact at work and at home.

The model connects life and demonstrates that problems in one aspect of life can have consequences in others. Too much of a social life might lead to health problems, too many hours at work might lead to family pressures and rising levels of frustration can easily lead to dissatisfaction and a change in temperament. The age old mantra of 'balance and moderation' is not as quaint as might be first thought. A wellbeing formula for the fast paced, mobile, compliance driven, hand held, 24/7 world of today might be similar to times well past.

For us in schools

In the world of schools and the organisation behind schools there are certainly many unique considerations. The demands of education are complex and exacting. Surrounding any individual in a school from the principal to coordinator to class teacher to in-class support staff are a myriad of daily interactions that mean no one job title lays claim to having their individual wellbeing most affected by events. The model provides examples of potential layers of complexity that add to the wellbeing experience. Of course, there are offsets for many of these and not everyone is affected in quite the same way, however, the point is that within the three perspectives the profession has a set of unique considerations. These are acknowledged in the Additional Considerations.

> The demands of education are complex and exacting.

Wellbeing is important in schools for adults as well as students. Within wellbeing there is an element of the glue that binds and adds to the level of satisfaction and enjoyment all staff can enjoy. Rising levels of wellbeing increase morale, mobilising people and rousing in them resources and skills they might not have thought existed.

Perhaps the worst aspect to wellbeing in schools is that given the general busyness, people simply get used to living with decreasing levels of wellbeing. We can become comfortable with the conditions around us and fail to see those ingrained habits and unproductive routines that serve us poorly. The advantage of a holistic model is to see this from a wider perspective, not just from the class or office level.

None of this is a particularly modern phenomenon. In 1649 William Harvey* made the crucial link between afflictions of the mind and the response of the heart. He was neatly and correctly describing the connection between the mind and the heart, a connection much studied today.

Individual reflection

- Are there 'out of balance' aspects to your life that cause some personal instability or increased personal worry?
- In what areas can you do more/do less to bring about a better balance to life?
- What are you mindful of from the model and what will you take care to foster?

*William Harvey is a fascinating historical character. He was born in 1578 and died in 1657. Harvey studied medicine in Cambridge and Padua in Italy. He was a staunch supporter of the monarchy and the physician to both James I and Charles I. The publication date above relates to his central work. He is likely to have made his discovery of circulation around 1618-1619.

👥 Staff conversation

- What are the offsets mentioned that are in place (or could be in place) to assist the wellbeing of employees? (support staff in classrooms, additional planning time, access to support groups, curriculum expertise)
- How effectively are we using the people resources already available to us?
- How do we describe the school climate and what can be done to improve climate, morale or relationships?

🔥 One step further

- Stress should not be seen as a pejorative term. 'It does not make sense that stress should always be a bad, harmful, negative entity' (Firduas Dhabhar quoted in Cox, D., Why everyday stress could be the key to a healthy old age, 2023). Dhabhar and others have shown that bouts of short term stress can aid us in the modern world through the production of chemicals in the blood that activate the immune system.
- The challenge is to think about stress in a different way. When has a degree of work stress resulted in an outcome of which you are genuinely proud? Think about a time where you had complex challenges, difficult conversations and taxing problems to solve but in the end achieved a durable and well received outcome.
- Where it is possible to take an individual response, use the model provided to improve your circumstances by working on two or three areas from the perspectives over a defined period of time. For example, for the next month you might like to concentrate your personal energies on (i) changing your night bed time routine to get more sleep (psychological perspective), (ii) lessen the amount of work taken home each night (lifestyle workstyle perspective), (iii) seriously look at your present exercise regime and adjust up (or down if the case may be). These are all individual choices based on your personal situation and recognising that changing our habits is never as easy as it sounds.

EPISODE 2

How do I build my capacity?

TITLE

How do I build my capacity?

FOCUS

 Individual Leader

 Leadership Team

 School community

WHY READ THIS

Positive, self reflective people want to improve. They are up for the next challenge and what they can learn. This episode will help you understand the important steps on the way.

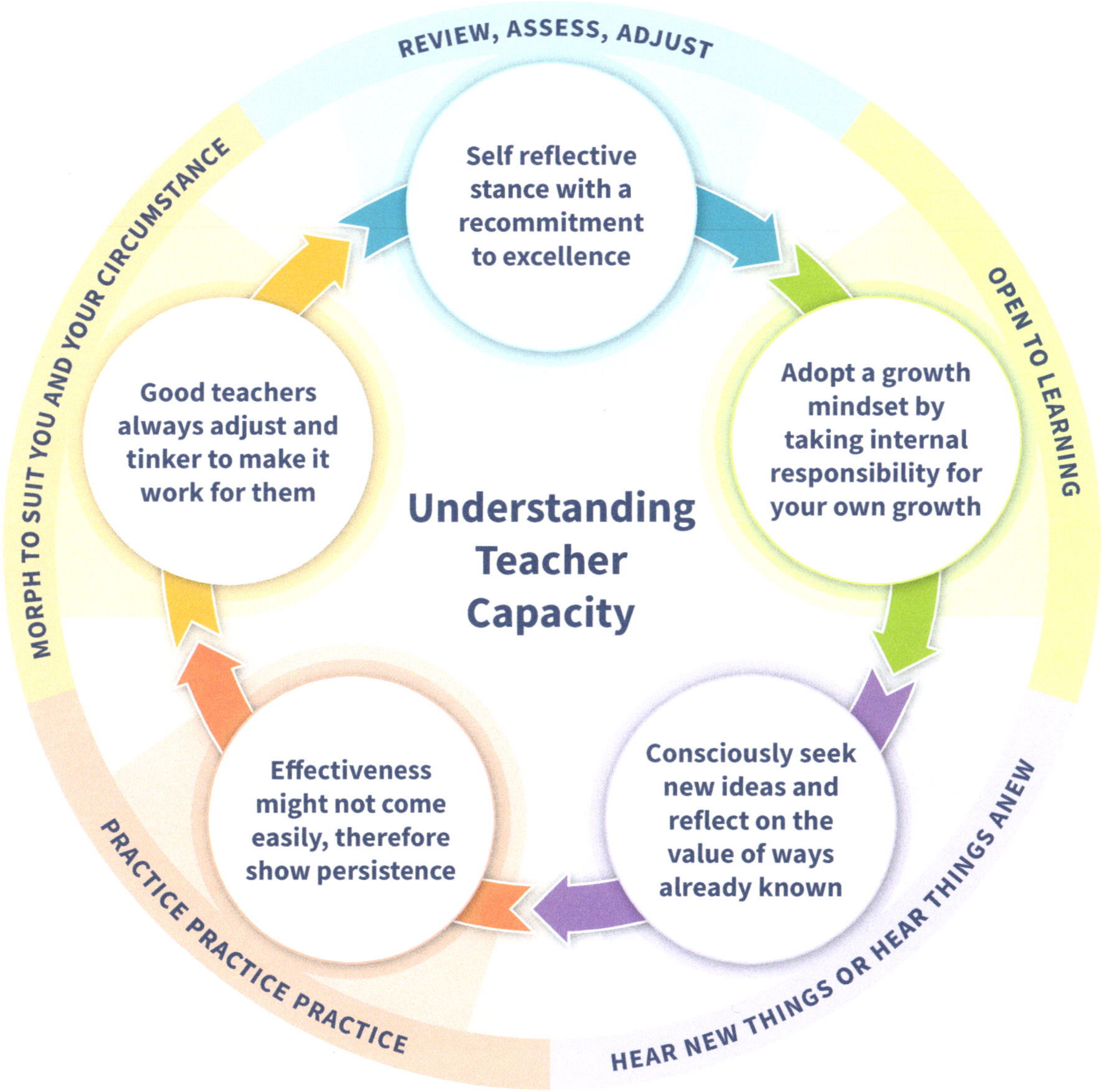

Understanding Teacher Capacity

- **REVIEW, ASSESS, ADJUST** — Self reflective stance with a recommitment to excellence
- **OPEN TO LEARNING** — Adopt a growth mindset by taking internal responsibility for your own growth
- **HEAR NEW THINGS OR HEAR THINGS ANEW** — Consciously seek new ideas and reflect on the value of ways already known
- **PRACTICE PRACTICE PRACTICE** — Effectiveness might not come easily, therefore show persistence
- **MORPH TO SUIT YOU AND YOUR CIRCUMSTANCE** — Good teachers always adjust and tinker to make it work for them

How do I build my capacity?

Two significant questions for any teacher should be:

1. How do I improve? And
2. How do I know I am improving?

Forward looking schools understand the concept of continuous improvement. That is, a restless desire to constantly challenge self and others to ensure we are all improving student academic and wellbeing outcomes. The notion that teacher capacity is fixed is incorrect. Everyone has the ability to improve. Capacity can be deliberately nurtured and formed by both the organisation (school and system together) through formal professional learning and by the individual through natural maturation led by curiosity.

The answer to the question 'how do I improve?' is found first in an individual's desire to learn. The psychologist Carol Dweck writes about how our mindset shapes the way we approach learning opportunities. Dweck proposes two mindsets, fixed and growth. Ezard explains the two mindsets this way: "Clarifying what growth really looks like and the internal approach we need to take to tackle challenges, obstacles and change is key to developing culture. When we move to action, we attempt new things, tackle obstacles and persist with challenges. Growth beliefs help people see obstacles and challenges as opportunities to be flexible and adaptable" (Ezard, 2015, p18).

Mindsets are powerful shapers of our experience, but people are not born with them. They develop through one's interactions with others, particularly in learning situations and in the feedback and exchanges one receives in those situations. "Our mindset develops through the subtle messages we encounter in classrooms and from teachers, mentors and parents" (Ritchhart, 2015, p57).

> Poor classroom and leadership practices fail students. Overcoming this is the one constant challenge facing us. Fixed mindsets with an inability to self evaluate exacerbate the problem.

The model presented in this Episode supports the notion of challenge and growth. None of us are overly tested by the same material endlessly repeated. To be really challenged we need to experience new things or see things anew.

A hard to hear message

Hattie's message (quoted in DuFour & Marzano, 2011, p16) might be simple, but nonetheless it is possibly difficult to hear. None of us would like to think we are average teachers (or worse), but the reality is, some of us might well be.

The message is simple – what teachers do matters. However, this has become a cliché that masks the fact that the greatest source of variance in our system relates to teachers – they can vary in many ways. The codicil is that what "some" teachers do matters…. The current mantra is that teachers make the difference…. This message like most simple solutions, is not quite right…. Not all teachers are effective, not all teachers are experts, and not all teachers have powerful effects on students.

A professional teacher should be able to self-reflect on their performance and make personal commitments on where they need to improve by changing or ceasing ineffective teaching practices. Sometimes we need assistance to realise this, sometimes we can see it in ourselves. How we respond to the realisation is always revealing. The same proposition applies to the collective staff and to the system itself.

Focusing on improving teacher growth and capacity has a direct line of sight to the improvement of the whole system. A study of the world's best-performing school systems concluded, "The quality of an education system cannot exceed the quality of its teachers" (Barber & Mourshed, 2007, p4).

Principals play an important role in the improvement of teacher capacity. Robinson (2018, p9) states that outsiders often "focus on the quality of the school leadership". While such quality is, of course, only one of multiple in-school and out-of-school influences on student achievement, it is the second most important, after teaching quality as the main in-school influence on student outcomes (Leithwood et al., 2006).

Nearly every evaluation of school improvement will partially attribute its degree of success to the quality of leadership (Robinson & Timperley, 2007). Leadership is the enabler of improvement, orchestrating the various conditions, such as professional capability, community engagement, and quality instruction, that need to be working together if improvement in student outcomes is to be achieved and sustained" (Bryk et al., 2015).

The capacity model

There is no real starting point in the capacity model. Like any virtuous circle there is no real beginning or end and improvements are both incremental and sustained. The basis of success is an open and inquiring mind (open to learning) and a willingness to persist. Hence the 'practice, practice, practice' mantra. Not everything comes easily and sometimes it just takes time to get it right. We all know those teachers or leaders who have that persistence trait. They do not let matters rest, be it supporting the less than effective teacher or implementing a new strategy across the school.

Teachers who consciously build their capacity often take on the new pedagogy/ technique/routine with a twist. They tinker and play with the idea to get it to suit their personality and pedagogical approach. While conformity and prescription are worthy concepts, so too are adaptation and difference. This of course, within agreed bounds. The point is that fine teachers know how to adapt material and work to their strengths.

And at all points in the circle, the best of the profession are constantly reviewing, assessing and adjusting their thinking, performance, attitude and practices. To assist them to do this they rely on trusted others, they value feedback, they analyse the data and they have a capacity to self evaluate.

Individual reflection

- Identify an occasion where you took an idea, concept or model from elsewhere and modified it to better suit your style, needs and class situation?
- Why are teachers often high self-markers? How do we truly see the gaps in our own performance?
- Have you ever spoken up about poor pedagogical practice within the school? How did you manage this delicate situation?
- Who assists you to reflect on personal practice? Can you identify recent feedback that made you think twice about your approach?

 Staff conversation

- Can we identify a recent occasion related to learning and student performance where everyone moved to action, tackled the obstacles and persisted in the teaching challenge? What was the group mindset in this case?
- What do you understand about the place of leadership in building teacher capacity?

One step further

- Do you have a 'trusted other?' This is a colleague who understands the role you are in and provides you with trusted and confidential advice about your beliefs and performance. They do so in direct but respectful, non-judgemental ways, mindful that it is a perspective only and that they are not your supervisor. A trusted other is not necessarily a friend or someone with whom you socialise. It may not be a reciprocal relationship either. The best 'trusted others' are the persons whose thinking and insights give you real pause for thought. You ask them questions and talk through scenarios openly. You value their opinion because you know they have something to offer you in understanding the situation. They can challenge your view of yourself and do not necessarily agree with everything you say. The best part about this relationship is that you use them to build your capacity.
- Finally, read more about the value of tinkering in: Invent to Learn - Martinez, S.L & Stager, G (2019)

EPISODE 3

TITLE

Understanding my motivation

FOCUS

 Individual Leader

 Leadership Team

 School community

WHY READ THIS

Every now and then it is a worthwhile activity to stop and reflect on personal attitudes and beliefs and share those reflections with a trusted colleague to obtain some added perspective. People are attracted to those whose values and opinions are quite obviously in alignment. This is amplified when they speak about possibilities with coherence, passion and enthusiasm.

Understanding my motivation

What do you know of, think of or believe about…

1. School Improvement and the emphasis on better results

2. Catering for diverse learners in the classroom

3. The use of data as evidence of learning

4. Working with other colleagues in my classroom

5. The emphasis on compliance and student safety

5 Things I Live By

1.
2.
3.
4.
5.

Understanding my motivation

If you are engaging with this material chances are you have been around education for some time and have seen enough of good and poor leadership to reflect meaningfully on your own performance and motivations.

Why did you choose teaching as a career in the first place? Quite possibly it was because your own experience of schooling was positive and you felt a strong desire to contribute to society and to connect meaningfully with people. Daniel Pink's book 'Drive: The surprising truth about what motivates us', (2009), helps us better understand our motivations and the secrets to performance and satisfaction in all aspects of life. 'Drive' is a good companion read and extension to this Episode. He turns on its head a number of traditional views including that money (with some caveats) and organisational goals are the keys to motivation. Many of us chose teaching as a way to express our human need to contribute in positive ways.

Every now and then it is a worthwhile activity to stop and reflect on personal attitudes and beliefs and share those reflections with a trusted colleague to obtain some added perspective. No matter how sharp we believe our thinking is, it is always better to speak it out loud and see how it sounds to others. Writing things down and saying them out loud to others always clarifies our thinking.

This four part Episode is intended to be used as a paired or group reflection. In these times of challenge and confusion it is helpful to clarify our thinking. A life in education and leadership offers many detours, false promises and unintended consequences that muddle our thinking and distract us from our goals. Every now and then we need to refocus.

In four parts

The first part centres on Your Story. Who and what has shaped you as a person and an educator and how has that changed over time? The second part of this Episode encourages you to think about what's important to you by asking 'What do you live by?' Our life is more than just a paid job. In the intense world of education an integrated life demands both perspective and balance. The third part in this Episode focuses on the present environment and its particular challenge by looking at the bigger picture. The fourth part challenges you to rediscover your passion by asking some high level leadership questions you might receive in an interview.

The intention of this Episode is to assist the reader know and express themselves and their convictions, motivations and personal philosophies. People are attracted to those whose values and opinions are quite obviously in alignment. This is amplified when they speak about possibilities with coherence, passion and enthusiasm.

First part: Your Story

Understand yourself first. Here are four reflective activities that can be used with a staff or in a group situation.

1. Can you list your first 7 teachers from primary school? Write their names down and circle just one name. Why did you circle that particular person? Hopefully it is for an honourable reason so explain why this person stands tall for you. It's always interesting to ask yourself why, after so many years, do you still remember this person and who will remember you in 30 years?

2. When did you 'grow up' as a teacher? At what moment in time or at what particular event did it dawn on you that there was a moral purpose to this career? Many of us are enthusiastic to start and at some point realise that enthusiasm must be tempered with the science behind teaching.

3. What did a parent tell you about success in life? That's probably some time ago but worth going back in time to see if it still holds out as true in your chosen career. How have you lived up to that advice over the years?

4. And finally, how have you changed over the years as a teacher? What do you find easier to forgive or harder to forgive in your colleagues? What would you never do now that once was commonplace?

Why we entered teaching in the first place might remain true and stay with us, however there is no doubt that we are also moulded by time, study, experience, professional learning and the colleagues with whom we work.

Second part: Five Things I Live By

A simple activity to encourage the group to talk.

This activity encourages professional conversation by focusing on what is really important in life to people. It is always a good idea to consider your own response before launching into this activity.

Often just breaking the ice and getting people conversing freely can be hard work especially when the main topic requires good levels of interaction and a degree of openness. This type of activity can bring a welcome burst of related conversation.

Introduce the activity perhaps by offering some personal insights, hand out the blank card with the heading; '5 Things I live by' and allow sufficient time for people to consider their response. In the follow up feedback session those willing might elaborate on their particular response. Try to find some commonalities across the group and any links to the day's work ahead of the group.

Sample responses have included:

Meditation, daily prayer, exercise, reading good literature, time with family and friends, no technology at the table, participating in community activity, stop and think before responding, phone mum each day, speak well of others, use your manners, talk less listen more, draw a line in the sand and move on….

A good extension activity is to draw from the group how these five statements relate to the work we do as educators. While not specifically education related, it might well be that a number of these statements relate to how we work together. In what ways are they important to us in teaching?

Useful variations of the above activity include:

- Five things I believe about students
- Five things I believe about successful classrooms
- Five things I believe about assessment

Third part: The bigger picture

There is no doubt the bigger picture can be quite distressing for many educators today. There are many trends and directions that on face value most of us have little disagreement with including, a strong push for school improvement, the use of advanced IT systems, the use of data as evidence, plain English reporting, safety compliance measures, a desire for uniformity, referencing the curriculum, recognising and catering for diverse learners, the use of national standards and guidelines and so on.

These are all worthy and just objectives. The disagreeable part for some is often not the concept, but the wider implications such as the overcrowding of the curriculum, the additional burdens placed on teachers, the implementation of the proposal or the possibility of negative school or individual comparisons.

Those in school leadership positions are caught between the system and the teachers, between knowing the intent and seeing the result, between supporting and defending. School leaders need to have a nicely tuned moral compass, a language that inspires and calms and an attitude that models possibilities.

To do this successfully it is important to understand your motivations.

Clarify your thinking. Construct a mind map using up to 10 short statements against each factor. The statements could include positives and negatives, what you like or dislike about the factor, problems with or advantages of etc. Do this activity reasonably promptly before sharing with a colleague. The factors are somewhat broad to enable you to explore your thinking more extensively. Here are some suitable examples to get you started:

- **School improvement and the emphasis on better results**
  Positives/ negatives, like/dislike, problems/advantages
- **Collecting student data as evidence of learning**
  Positives/ negatives, like/dislike, problems/advantages
- **Catering for diverse learners in the classroom**
  Positives/ negatives, like/dislike, problems/advantages
- **Working with other colleagues in my classroom**
  Positives/ negatives, like/dislike, problems/advantages
- **The emphasis today on compliance and student safety**
  Positives/ negatives, like/dislike, problems/advantages

When sharing, take the time to jointly explore the intellectual depth of the issues you are raising. These are weighty matters and they deserve the time to explore. Make sure you include in the conversation:

- The commonalities between you and your partner and where the emphasis is in each mind map.
- Your position on the issue. Can you speak to your position in this factor concisely and passionately without saying phrases like '*you know what I mean,…*? How do you ensure others understand the nuance of your thinking?
- What has caused you to change your position over time?
- How do you negotiate the pressure to deliver from the system or employer with the 'on the ground' reality of an overworked and underappreciated staff?

Keep the mind maps and adjust them as the conversation flows.

The fourth part: Rediscover your passion for leadership

Presenting for a job interview can be a nerve wracking, tricky business but it forces us to confront some basic motivational questions. We know the first question will be 'why are you applying' as a starter. There can't be many people who enjoy the prospect, particularly when other aspects of life such as paying the mortgage hinge off the success or otherwise of the interview. Job interviews are competitive, often unforgiving and serious matters. But, let's look at this another way.

In this final exercise, don't just answer the job interview questions in your head and congratulate yourself on another well constructed killer response. Rather, find a colleague and ask them to ask you, in a mock interview style, the questions or variations of the questions and observe yourself in the response. Similarly to the other exercises in this Episode, it is in the saying out loud that we see the more obvious gaps in our explanations and understanding. Here are a number of interview questions to consider, all based on real life interviews.

With a colleague in a serious mock interview format answer these questions:

- What does a high performance culture look like?
- What's your educational point of difference? What do you stand on?
- What will you not stand for in teacher behaviour?
- How do you turn a complainant into a supporter?
- How do you manage the disparity between the staff minimalists and the staff expansionists?
- One year's teaching should equal one year's growth. How do you measure that?
- How do you show people joy, even when faced with great stress or adversity?
- How do you express your vulnerability in school life?
- Define success for you in your leadership?
- How do others see you that is different to the way you see yourself?

 Individual reflection

- What do you think motivates people to improve their pedagogy?
- How do you approach staff you think have lost their motivation?
- At the end of the day ask yourself, 'Was I better today than yesterday?'

 Staff conversation

- How can we personalise the school's goals to better suit our situation?
- How do we encourage more creativity and still remain true to the school's stated goals?

 One step further

- Read 'Drive: The surprising truth about what motivates us', (Pink, 2009).
- We expect students to have a growth mindset but what of ourselves? The fixed mindset says: "I can't do it". The growth mindset says: "I can't do it *yet*". What attitudes do you have to change to overcome a fixed mindset in a nominated aspect of school life. Make sure this commitment is reflected in your professional goals.

EPISODE 4

Conducting a professional conversation

TITLE

Conducting a professional conversation

FOCUS

 Individual Leader

 Leadership Team

 School community

WHY READ THIS

Conversations about practice occur within the context of the school's culture so both are directly linked. Poorly conducted conversations lead quickly to negative cultural impacts. The proper tone, the right words, the best setting and thoughtful preparation are essential to your success.

1. Think back to a recent professional conversation
2. Choose a conversation of substance where there was a real need to talk
3. Consider your motivation, response to the other person, the outcomes
4. Step through the conversation in a self-reflective way using the 10 steps

5. **Clarity**. How did you establish understanding early on?

6. **Good faith**. How did you set up the tone of the meeting? What language was used to indicate your approach?

7. **Body language**. How were you conscious of your own body position and gesture response throughout the meeting?

8. **Two-way conversation**. What did you do to ensure the conversation was back and forth? How did you stop yourself over talking?

9. **Distractions**. How did you ensure distractions were managed?

10. **On task**. Were you able to keep the conversation on track? Did you have to return to the agreed purpose?

11. **Questioning.** How would you describe your use of questions? Were you satisfied with your general approach and tone? Did you get to the heart of the matter

12. **Meta thinking.** As the conversation progressed, did you observe yourself and assess the direction of the meeting?

13. **Boundaries**. Were there boundaries to be recognised in the conversation that might affect possible outcomes? If so, were you satisfied with how they were expressed and understood?

14. **Agreement/resolution**. Was this a necessary element in the conversation? Did you reach a satisfactory outcome? Rate your success in finding a resolution.

Conducting a professional conversation

One of the most basic occurrences in any school situation is the professional conversation with a colleague. This Episode is concerned with those conversations where a concern is raised.

The effective functioning of any school depends on a constant back and forth conversation between adults. The quality of the conversations, particularly when concerns are raised, will put the school's culture on full display. Professional conversations in this Episode are treated differently to the more formal performance conversations. Any conversation with a bite will be related to someone's concern. An expressed concern may develop into a formal performance process, however, for the purposes of this Episode the content is related to addressing the initial concern through professional conversation.

One of the principal characteristics of a learning organisation is that everyone accepts the obligations to engage in ongoing professional learning and that teaching is challenging and complex work that is impossible to do perfectly (Danielson, C, Talk about Teaching, 2016, p69-73).

The timely resolution of concerns is central to a school's success. 'Concerns' is an interesting word and need not always be high level, high stakes, emotional matters. Almost always, concerns will be about people and relationships, although issues around resourcing and policy and procedure can be factors.

Concerns are not, in and of themselves, entirely undesirable since they have the potential to prompt efforts to positive change.... But their persistence is likely to undermine the goals of instructional leadership (Robinson et al., 2016, p27).

There are scores of times in the week where information needs to be discussed, plans made, confidences shared, apologies made, misunderstandings sorted and agreements reached. There are different levels of seriousness, hierarchies to be accounted for, personal agendas to be respected or not and implications for others in these conversations.

Done poorly, these daily interactions will result in a deteriorating culture.

What can go wrong? (Plenty)

At our worst we are consumed by power, prestige and our position in the organisation and it is never easy to put these aside. Most times we want to be right and unfortunately sometimes we want to show the other party how wrong they are. We can cover up our true intentions and we often downplay our emotions saying things like, 'I'm not worried about'… or we frame it up as someone else's concern. Sometimes we express ourselves poorly in response to the person who brought the complaint. If we are new to the situation, perhaps we haven't yet seen the full extent of the bigger picture and we act with limited information. Overcoming these common dispositions and human traits requires mature conversations which demand the emotional maturity of both parties.

Danielson (2016, p69-73) identifies these factors as important to ensure the success of the interaction: conversational tone, linguistic skills (questioning techniques), rapport (tone and body language) and how thinking is encouraged. Asking powerful questions in a safe environment leads to people thinking about their practice.

The question of trust is also implicit in a mature conversation. While we all like to think ourselves trustworthy and our motivations pure, the other party may hold a very different view to our own. Looking in the mirror is not helpful as we only see ourselves reflected back. A most important aspect to trust is the quality of the daily interactions held with others in the school. Our personal regard for others, level of interest in their affairs, listening ability and follow up actions all contribute to building up high levels of trust. Almost everything in schools is relational.

How do you conduct yourself when you have a parent complaint, a strong pedagogical position to declare, a stake in the outcome or a future to consider? How do you manage people on staff at odds with each other? How do you converse with central office staff who have a particular view which might be different to yours?

> A most important aspect to trust is the quality of the daily interactions held with others in the school.

Conducting a professional conversation

These 10 steps will help.

1. Find clarity to avoid possible misunderstandings during the conversation and later on by first asking 'What are we hoping to achieve today?'

2. Emphasise that we are together today in good faith to seek understanding of the other's position. That is, a conversation that is honest in belief, purpose and intention. Highlight that this is valued time and we want to make the most of the conversation.

3. Depending on the situation and as best you can, be at ease with the person particularly if there is a power imbalance. Adopt a neutral face, good body posture and smile as appropriate.

4. Make this a two way conversation, balanced in terms of who is speaking so it becomes a back and forth conversation. Those with an authority or leadership role must be mindful of not 'taking over', dictating terms or being judgemental.

5. Keep distractions and interruptions from outside away. Simple things like phones off make a difference in the atmosphere. Move away from screens and focus on the person.

6. Be mindful of conversational detours coming into the conversation. Keep to the purpose and remind the other person what is to be achieved here today. Expand the conversation if necessary but stay fixed on the agreed goal.

7. Questioning is a skill. The quality of the questioning of each other and its tone will assist in coming to better understand the other's position. This is not a TV political interview, no one is trying to ask the 'gotcha' question or expose weakness in the argument as a way of demonstrating intellectual superiority. Genuine questions do not seek to reinforce the questioner's point of view.

8. As best you can try and observe yourself and the flow of the conversation during the meeting. The meta cognitive aspect is important because it can assist in bringing matters back on track if they start to go awry. Always be asking yourself 'have I struck the right tone', is this meeting the other person's needs?' Check for understanding as the meeting progresses and particularly after any exchange that brought some additional emotion to the surface.

9. At some point in the meeting, and best early on in the conversation because it links to the first question, there needs to be a recognition of boundaries, chiefly being: procedural/policy matters to be observed, authority limits, budget constraints, flexibility limits or unique circumstances. This is not to limit the outcome or constrain the conversation but to keep it legitimate, realistic and within the bounds of the possible.

10. If this is a necessary element in the conversation and related to the purpose, find an agreement, accommodation or agree on further exploration and conversations. Summarising and finding common ground towards the end of the conversation brings closure. Depending on the seriousness, write up and share the agreement.

> Why ask a question when we know the answer? Why ask a question to stump the other person? Why ask a question so we look good?

🔆 Individual reflection

- What (i) do people tell you are your conversational strengths and (ii) do you know of yourself that needs to improve in conversations of substance?
- Recall a recent conversation where you had to meta think about your approach within the conversation. Why was this the case?
- How do you put aside power, prestige and position in the conversation to put the other party at ease?

👥 Staff conversation

- As a staff how do we understand the importance of appropriate and insightful questioning? When do we practice such questioning with each other?

🔥 One step further

There is plenty of scope in this Episode for improvement for everyone. Good conversational skills are never 'set and forget'. We must always be mindful of conversational tone, linguistic skills (questioning techniques), rapport (tone and body language) and how thinking is encouraged. Ask a trusted colleague to take you through a recent particularly intense professional conversation. Use the graphic to fully analyse the interaction. When you are going through this conversation try to separate out facts and feelings. Some questions to ask yourself are:

- What might have been said by you in a better way?
- What was my balance of speaking and listening in this conversation?
- Did your feelings get in the way at any point? (That is your emotional reaction to what was said)
- Did you miss the opportunity for a useful question at any point?
- How aware were you of facial expressions, body language and excessive note taking?

EPISODE 5

TITLE

Marks of a teacher leader

FOCUS

 Individual Leader

 Leadership Team

 School community

WHY READ THIS

If you are a teacher interested in promoting instructional or learning leadership in the school, or if you have teachers you wish to develop and promote in this way, this Episode will assist in understanding the professional attributes of these invaluable staff.

Marks of a teacher leader

Use these questions as a personal reflection tool. Teacher leaders are learners because they are curious, open minded, and interested in others' success. If the response is a YES or a NO, add in reasons why this might be the case for you. Answer honestly; what's the point of doing otherwise?

Collaborative

- Do I clarify any misunderstandings with others quickly?
- Do I talk to a wide variety of people at work (or just stay within my comfortable group)?
- How am I supporting the initiatives of others?
- How do I connect with the leadership team?
- How do I show I value collective wisdom?
- How do I show my disappointment when it doesn't go my way?
- Are my conversations with colleagues and parents building trust and understanding?

Learner

- What do I know of how people say I present myself?
- Do I ask people questions in warm and encouraging ways?
- How do I demonstrate I am a learner to others?
- How do people know I'm listening?
- How do I show I value professional learning?
- How do I demonstrate I can translate theory into everyday practice?
- How well do I know the syllabus?
- What professional texts am I reading?

Outward

- How well connected professionally am I?
- When did I last converse professionally with a colleague from elsewhere?
- In what ways do I show that I foster and value the whole team?
- How connected am I with people in other schools?
- When was the last time I was in another school for a *Learning Walk and Talk* type visit?
- How do I demonstrate I'm focused on others and not just me?
- How effective are my social media feeds in presenting me with new ideas and fresh thinking?

Consistency

Am I where I say I'll be?

Do I follow up as I promise?

How do I really know how I am going? Who tells me?

How do I feel about changing my mind?

Am I clear with what I'm looking for when talking with others?

How do people know I'm in this for the long haul?

Curious about students

Do I talk with students about their work?

When observing students am I conscious of their engagement with the work?

How do I organise and value the evidence of student learning?

Are my conversations with colleagues about student growth and potential?

Am I sufficiently knowledgeable about data and its uses to the point where I can talk about data confidently?

Simplify

Do I express my thoughts as well in words as in my head?

How do I find ways to translate the message into understandable language?

Can I retell things in different ways?

Am I focused on the big picture?

How do I prevent the small details (overly) crowding my thinking?

Is my writing clear to others?

Joyous

How do I show I'm interested in others?

What gives me joy in school life?

How do I show my delight about improved student performance?

How will others see my growth mindset?

Do I laugh regularly with others?

How do I foster trust?

How do I know I'm a warm and inviting person?

Curious about teachers and teaching

Do I watch others and consciously think 'I could try that'?

Have I ever tested completely new ideas with colleagues?

How do I know I've hit the mark with a new classroom process?

When was the last time I changed course because it wasn't working?

How do I show real interest in others' work?

Do I talk more than I listen?

Marks of a teacher leader

Improving teacher quality is a focus in all education systems because it is the pathway to student success, better educational outcomes for the school and stronger student and staff wellbeing.

The term 'teacher leader' in this context refers to those in the profession who are either in the classroom full time and actively engaging with others or close to the classroom supporting teachers directly with their work. Teacher leaders can therefore be in recognised roles (such as an Instructional Coach, Leader of Pedagogy or similar) or they can be full time classroom teachers with a passion for sharing practice and engaging with others.

Strong teacher leaders can help us all regain the enthusiasm and creativity we need to build stronger schools. Teacher leaders do more than educate students. They model for everyone what it is to be a true learner. Teacher leaders educate the whole school and play a particularly important role in promoting the curriculum through their enthusiasm, results, creativity and collaborative skills.

And one particular attribute of vital importance is competency. Kirtman defines competency as, an observable behaviour that demonstrates skills, learning and experience (2013, p5).

The most valuable resource for any education system is its human capital and the continued growth of that capital. A broader element in this improvement agenda is the need to provide suitable pathways for emerging teacher leaders to assist others in the continuous development of their craft. This is also true at the school level.

There are many frameworks, models and approaches that look to building teacher leaders. Without such teacher leaders who operate close to and in the classroom and who take a personal interest in the pedagogical development of others, the school would be a much poorer place. Many will go on to be the next generation of formal school leaders. Others, hopefully, choose to stay in or close to the classroom. They bring an energy that impacts in positive ways by building the human capital in the school. Teacher leaders encourage thinking, reflection and good practice.

> Pedagogy must be a deliberate, strategic and mindful choice because it has profound consequences. Pedagogy reflects the type of learning, learners, schools and society we want to create. Pedagogy contributes to defining not only teachers, but to defining who learners are and can be.
> (Jefferson and Anderson, 2017, p48)

The place of the APST

Teachers will find *The Australian Professional Standards for Teachers (ASPT)* an excellent resource. The Standards are also a good way to think about what improved teacher capacity means. There is no doubt that a teacher's effectiveness is the single most important factor influencing student achievement. Better teachers equals better outcomes. Teachers who are striving for excellence by adopting an attitude of continuous improvement are a dependable and consistent influence on the students in their care.

The Standards are intended to attract, develop, recognise and retain quality teachers. The categories of Highly Accomplished and Lead Teacher provide the pathway to grow as a professional. The Australian Professional Standards for Teachers comprise seven Standards that outline what teachers should know and be able to do. The Standards are interconnected, interdependent and overlapping. The Standards are grouped into three domains of teaching: Professional Knowledge, Professional Practice and Professional Engagement. Each of these three domains can be used to illustrate growth: increased knowledge, improved practice and better engagement. The Australian Professional Standards for Teachers provides an excellent framework for teacher leaders to develop their skills in a researched and systematic way.

Finding the time to think

In Creating Cultures of Thinking (2015, p3) Ron Ritchhart asks: 'When and where have you been a part of a culture of thinking? That is, when have you been in a place where the group's (let us say a school staff) collective thinking as well as everyone's thinking was valued, visible and actively promoted as part of the regular day-to-day experience of all group members?' This is a simple but surgical question. Many people are happy to talk, fewer are happy to listen and reflect on their own practice and perhaps then talk.

Bezzina's reflections on system capacity building have a parallel when considering the role of teacher leaders within the individual school. Bezzina challenges school leaders to share emerging wisdom with others, 'noticing and amplifying', taking the pollen of good ideas and innovative and effective practice to nurture growth and capacity (2018, p150). What better role for an 'inhouse' teacher leader than to be the pollinator so that best practice can be shared and amplified, intentionally and regularly.

Competencies of teacher leaders

Teacher leaders promote a thinking culture. They see learning as a social activity in the sense that it should, if not be fun, at least be a pleasant experience. Their mindset is one of open to learning. They are naturally joyous people who are more interested in others than in themselves. The questions in the graphic offer a personal reflection to those who wish to contribute to the profession through a closer connection with colleagues.

Additionally, the following characteristics have been identified by Kirtman as competencies for high performing leaders:

- Challenges the status quo
- Builds trust through clear communication and expectations
- Creates a commonly owned plan for success
- Focuses on team over self
- Creates a high sense of urgency for change and sustainable results
- Commits to continuous self improvement
- Builds external networks and partnerships (Kirtman, 2013).

High performing teacher leaders share many of these competencies. They are not exclusively for principal leadership.

Problems to be overcome

A teacher leader will have a variety of relationships within the school. These relationships might be formal, informal, one-on-one or working with a group of colleagues. A formal relationship might be defined as coaching or mentoring. Sometimes these are paid, contracted positions (such as a literacy coach), other times the teacher leader is the classroom teacher.

In the informal sense, a teacher leader might be a person who works full time in a class but who exerts influence on others in positive ways through the combination of their outward, engaging personality and high level pedagogical skills.

While there are inherent differences between the formal and the informal, most teachers are well aware of the concept and practice of both. Be it a formal or informal relationship both types exert a positive influence on those around them. These staff members are about professional growth. When we are at our best we are open to new thinking, accepting of advice, keen to question and process what we've heard and want to be better at what we do.

Anderson and Cawsey provide a list of commonly experienced problems for both the mentor and mentee. They provide insights into how to overcome the issue to ensure the best effects are achieved.

Problem experienced	For mentor	For mentee
Lack of time to meet	X	X
Professional expertise/ personality mismatch	X	X
Lack of proximity to each other	X	X
Unrealistic expectations from the relationship	X	X
Perceptions of an unequal status (such as the mentor knew it all; mentee expressed own ideas)	X	X
Conflicting mentor role - advice vs assessment	X	
Emotionally draining or too stressful	X	
Colleagues feeling jealous	X	
An added responsibility and a burden	X	
Inadequate preparation of mentor – clarity of role, skills, goals (2008, p33)	X	X

Adequate preparation before commencing, careful people matching, ongoing training, professional supervision and regular review will overcome most of these identified issues. That said, all the above are common enough failures in such engagements so to be most effective, take note of the potential problems before commencing the venture.

Individual reflection

- How do I ensure my results are sustainable and replicable in other classes?
- What am I 'noticing and then amplifying' in the school?
- How do I allow others to share their expertise with me?
- What am I reading at present that I can share with others?
- What are my special interests in the curriculum and with pedagogy?

Staff conversation

- How do we demonstrate that we are open to others being in our classroom?
- What better meeting structures are there for promoting curiosity about student learning?
- How can we better use system personnel to advance our thinking?

One step further

- If you are a school leader can you identify an existing class teacher with no additional responsibilities who might show signs of promise as a teacher leader. What can be done to encourage them to take a more active role in the school's pedagogical conversations? What opportunities are available for them to step up and contribute in a more public way?
- How does the school engage with the two higher levels of the Australian Professional Standards for Teachers? Are there teachers on staff who qualify for the levels but who may be reluctant to take the application steps? Whatever their reluctance may be (financial, family, current role, time as examples) what practical things can you do to assist them start the process?

EPISODE 6

TITLE

Managing expectations

FOCUS

 Individual Leader

 Leadership Team

 School community

WHY READ THIS

Effective responses to dissatisfaction, poor feedback or complaints is a constant challenge for every principal. The stark reality is that without consistently effective responses to managing expectations the school's reputation, culture and management is called into question by the community.

Managing expectations

- What motivated you to call me today?
- How can we improve the situation?
- What can I do to assist?
- How long has this been bothering you?

27

Managing expectations

As a principal, the management of community expectations is vital. It is true to say that these days peoples' view of any authority figure or institution is much diminished. Continuous attention to expectations by managing up is essential. Dealing effectively with dissatisfaction, poor feedback and complaints management are all part of the job. When no or an unsatisfactory response is forthcoming then the situation will deteriorate to the point where the school's reputation, culture and management is called into question by the community. The best response to managing expectations is a proactive response.

From the outset, this Episode does not have to be regarded as a negative or deficit based approach to leadership. The best leaders will always act ethically and fairly when dealing with persons presenting with dissatisfaction, poor feedback or complaints. They will not rely on crafty responses, showmanship or untruths to respond. Proactive leaders have structures and processes in place to minimise misunderstandings and properly manage expectations.

The importance of responding to and resolving dissatisfaction, poor feedback or complaints in a consistent, fair, just and effective way helps to create the conditions that allow relationships to lift to a new level. This cannot be understated. Leaders who can do this free up parent, individual and staff emotional energy giving relationships a better chance to thrive.

Regardless of the legitimacy of the dissatisfaction, poor feedback or complaint or not, oftentimes in such situations the complainant might be confused, angry, irrational or distracted. A careful approach and the right questions will allow for the listener to assist the complainant to get to the heart of the matter in an ordered way.

Some definitions

There are some subtle differences between the three terms used in this Episode. The Commonwealth Ombudsman's Better Practice Handling Guide defines complaint as:

'An implied or express statement of dissatisfaction where a response is sought, reasonable to expect or legally required.'

And feedback as:

'Feedback is a compliment, criticism, comment or suggestion where a response is not sought, or not reasonable to expect.'

The key difference between complaints and critical feedback is the reasonable expectation of a response. Like complaints, it is important to ensure that feedback can be analysed to identify opportunities for improvement.

Broader issues around managing expectations

There are many associated factors surrounding the management of dissatisfaction, poor feedback and complaints. For the purposes of this Episode they are grouped into these three headings: School structures and processes, People issues and Habits of thinking.

School structures and processes

Leaders who are attuned to preventative and proactive measures will be mindful of ensuring the school's complaint policy and practices in this general area are regularly reviewed and made fit for purpose. When this is in place, the speed and faithfulness of the response is more likely to be seen as positive by the community. Reactive responses will always be problematic when the response pathway or the policy is deficient. Reactive responses can easily reinforce peoples' view that the institution is hiding something, protecting someone or outright lying. Therefore, to be preventative and proactive when managing expectations ensure that:

- The school's (and the system's) complaint policy and processes for parents and staff is visible, easily available, quite clear and current. This includes being direct with parents and staff about the process for lodging a complaint and who will be dealing with the matter.

- The school's risk management practices are taken seriously. Acknowledging that potential conflicts can often be avoided by some simple advance steps especially when past experience is applied is important. Risk management is often seen by staff as burdensome and unnecessary. Nothing could be further from the truth.

- Follow up with those involved is conducted. Checking in regularly with the parties and closely observing relationships post complaint, acting to support or intervene where necessary so as to lower the pressure is important.

- The management of students in general by the staff, the use of positive behaviour techniques, the staffs' attitudes and response to student indiscretions and the respect for and the application of the school's rules is observed.
- Parent exit surveys are used to ensure leadership openness to seeing other perspectives.
- There is a strong focus on student safety, wellbeing and pastoral care.

People issues

While positive feedback is always welcomed, unfortunately some feedback will be negative. The management of expectations requires both leadership maturity and common sense. Matters can easily get out of control when people act in ways that are unhelpful. Alternatively, when people respond in helpful ways matters can be addressed with less emotion.

Some examples of the diverse range of possibilities in people issues might include:

- The known and unknown history of the complaint and whether the backstory has legitimacy.
- Staff communication practices, email and the use of social media.
- The actions of any 'influencers' on the staff including the principal's PA.
- The respect for confidentiality and the corrosive effect of gossip and rumour.
- Front desk welcome and the response abilities of those people whom the public first see or talk to, their attentiveness and respect for all people and the way they manage people.
- Principal availability, visibility and presence in the school particularly in places where people are congregating, interacting and engaged in the work of school.

Any of the above can be viewed in positive and negative ways. For example, a strong PA can be a great support for a principal when matters require close attention. Managing people is infinitely harder than managing anything else.

Habits of thinking

Leaders with emotional maturity can recognise and respond to some of the unhelpful habits of thinking that persons presenting with dissatisfaction, poor feedback or complaints might be prone. It is reasonable to assume there will be some strong opinions so be mindful of people:

- Seeing this matter in black and white terms: There are many shades of grey in school life. Oftentimes the full story is not quite as clear cut as some might wish.
- Catastrophising: The imagined outcome, however horrible it might sound, might never come to pass.
- Overgeneralising: Saying things like 'Every teacher does this…' or 'You always ..'.

Leaders who think about dissatisfaction, poor feedback and complaints in a balanced way manage expectations by:

- Avoiding unhelpful habits of thinking themselves.
- Accepting the person is acting in good faith.
- Remaining positive that a solution can be found.
- Advancing staff skill levels by engaging in professional learning and using consultant support available to build staff skills and knowledge.
- Modelling a mature perspective to others by acting in a temperate manner.
- Watching the use of social media and email and correcting any loose staff practices.

The use of open ended questions in these situations

Open ended questions avoid the YES or NO response. Open ended questions most often begin with Why, What and How. They promote deeper thinking and enable fuller responses. There is more chance of additional insight when listening to an open ended question response. For leaders faced with dissatisfaction, poor feedback or a complaint the use of open ended questions is encouraged.

Active listening is the key term. It is not unknown for principal respondents to seek to convince, talk over the top of, robustly defend, try and fix the problem quickly or deny responsibility. Deep listening requires some impulse control to avoid these common traps. Open ended questioning will allow for follow up questions or opportunities to request the respondent tell you more about a particular incident or reaction.

The use of the Why question requires some caution as it may trigger a defensive or aggressive response.

Some useful open ended questions

These open ended questions are intended to open up a dialogue which allows the respondent to listen first. This is best done with a non-judgemental stance, eye contact, relaxing hand gestures and facial expressions that don't suggest disbelief or antagonise the other party.

1. What motivated you to attend today?

This type of question gives a sense of the complainant's timeline and level of discomfort which allows for some professional judgement including how effective the school's feedback mechanisms might be. It is reasonable to ask the complainant why it had taken so long for the issue to come to the school's attention or alternatively, why it took so long to come to the principal's attention if a teacher knew of the matter well beforehand. This is a good example of open ended questions opening up further fruitful lines of questioning and understanding.

2. How do we stop this happening again?

Many people want you to solve the issue for them. While this may be entirely leadership's problem to solve, it may also be best attended to with a joint approach. This question puts the onus back on the complainant, by offering them the opportunity to suggest workable solutions themselves.

The respondent might well agree with the best way forward and could potentially offer suggestions and modifications. If there is no 'best way forward' forthcoming, the respondent might have to suggest their own solution but this is always the least preferred option. When agreed, the ownership and responsibility for moving forward becomes a shared responsibility.

3. How can we improve the situation?

The key word in this question is the use of 'we' as a way of suggesting a joint approach might be best. In any disagreement the parties involved might be seeking redress way beyond what is either possible or appropriate. For example, oftentimes complainants want people dismissed from employment. It's a good question to put to any complainant so that the respondent can reality check or support them if necessary.

Perhaps the outcomes sought are way beyond what is possible, appropriate or necessary. It is important to be quite clear as to what you will not do as well as what you will do in the situation.

4. Is there anything else I should know?

A useful 'catch all' question that offers the complainant the opportunity to address any other related matters. If there is tension, the best approach is to give the complainant the time needed to put all the issues on the table. There is nothing worse than hearing post meeting that the complainant felt rushed or limited in what they could say.

Alternatively, if the question is put and no additional information is offered, yet later it becomes known by the school that the complainant is raising other matters, then rightfully the school can suggest they were unaware.

5. How can we talk about this with your child?

The respondent may or may not know exactly what the complainant has done to date but in any case this open question puts the onus back on the person with the complaint to outline what might have been said at home.

The actions taken by the complainant might be appropriate (or inappropriate), effective (or ineffective). The respondent can applaud, make suggestions, redirect behaviour, provide some educational advice or if necessary be more direct. The question highlights the helpful and potentially unhelpful actions that may have been undertaken to date.

6. What are your expectations of people at school?

This type of question again allows the respondent to reality check or confirm with the complainant what they are able and willing to do (or not do as the case may be). The respondent can outline clear and unmistakable terms of engagement in this matter leaving no party in any doubt as to what will be done.

Without doubt the management of dissatisfaction, poor feedback or complaints is a key leadership function and will highlight the difference between leaders. It is important to note that a mature, balanced and calm approach in the face of hostility or disbelief is never easy.

 ## Individual reflection

- In what ways do you fall into the trap of solving problems for others rather than assisting them solve the problem for themselves?
- As a principal how often do you find yourself rushing to the answer, convincing others on a course of action or failing to consider all the alternatives?

 ## Staff conversation

- Is there anything in the list of school structures and processes that might deserve attention at school?

 ## One step further

A full review of the school's complaint management process is a significant job, however, it is one that might be worth the effort.

Listening skills are critical in complaint management. Like all skills they require regular maintenance and some occasional outside assistance. Ask a trusted colleague to observe an interaction (which may not be a complaint type interaction) where you and a colleague are engaged in weighty conversation.

Use this simple checklist and score card to record the observations. Conduct a post conversation debrief and discuss the use of the strategies.

Strategy	Tick number of times recorded	
Probing: asking clarifying questions		
Silence: using no voice, full attention, suitable body language		
Paraphrasing: rephrasing in your own words to ensure correct interpretation		
Summarising: bringing the conversation together		
Shifting the level of abstraction: Looking at the issue in a bigger picture way trying to take it away from the personal to diffuse the situation		

Parker, A., Peak Performance Development, Negotiators ToolKit, 2012. www.peakpd.com

School team focus summary map

E7 Next level team
In well performing schools working in teams is a given.

E8 Using data effectively
There is often plenty of evidence that could be used to make learning decisions and evaluate the effectiveness of different programs adopted in schools but the exercise is fraught with problems.

E9 Strong leadership teams and the underlying vision
Principals who foster trust, are well respected by others, act with integrity and have solid organisational skills are highly likely to have a leadership team in place that both supports and challenges their thinking.

E10 Hope is a strategy
A commonly heard, confidently stated statement is that 'hope is not a strategy', however, in certain conditions HOPE can be a very effective strategy.

E11 Getting started
New to a school or just wanting a fresh start? When there are countless frameworks and strategies to choose from it is difficult to know where to start.

E12 Changing things
A certainty about school is that change can be a problem. From the simple to the highly complex, change needs to be managed. So, how do we better cope with this certainty?

E13 My contribution
Forget about the others for a moment. What am I bringing to the culture of the leadership team? Is my contribution to this team building community and adding value through creative and consistent input? In this leadership team am I participating in the way that is expected of every other team member in this school?

These Episodes are intended for conversation within the team setting.

They are suited to any type of team and not limited to the Leadership Team (however defined by the school).

The arrows indicate a complementary relationship between Episodes in this focus area.

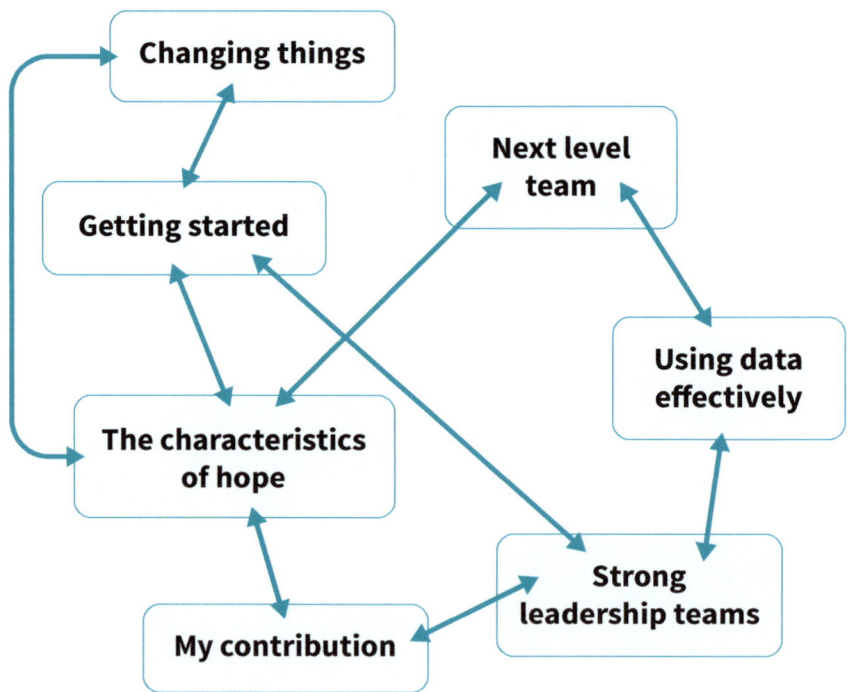

EPISODE 7

Next level team

TITLE

Next level team

FOCUS

 Individual Leader

 Leadership Team

 School community

WHY READ THIS

The success of the school rests on the strength of the teacher teams. School leaders need to understand how to set up the conditions for teams to experience learning growth themselves.

| 1ST LEVEL |
| 2ND LEVEL |
| 3RD LEVEL |

1st Level — At its most basic

- Teachers meet as a cohort on a routine, agreed basis
- Leadership members take a passing interest in the team
- Individual teams are not connected
- Teachers in a supporting role are invited to these meetings
- The focus is chiefly 'planning', tasks are allocated
- People attend to their jobs as agreed

Performance Note

- Ostensibly there are teams in place. This type of team is best characterised as a loose arrangement where strong personalities might dominate and challenging them is problematic.
- At Level 1 participation can be erratic particularly when persons engage only on topics that suit them and turn off (and turn on the technology) as it suits.
- Meeting formats are not structured so the loudest voices can lead the conversation. School specialists are only invited to the meetings, sometimes reluctantly.
- Across the school different rules are evident in these teams and there is no clearing house so understandings are not shared.
- The planning aspect is strong so the emphasis is on what to teach. People certainly do their jobs as agreed so things happen.
- Across the school some teams are more effective than others.

2nd Level — A step up

- Teachers meet as a year level and in other formats on a routine, agreed basis
- Leadership team members attend as appropriate
- Individual Teams are connected by a whole of school gathering or other agreed means that promotes communication
- A whole of school understanding of the purpose of these teams is in place
- Meeting norms are written and observed
- Teachers in a supporting role attend as equal partners
- The focus is on collaboration beyond planning the curriculum
- There is a strong pedagogical strand in the conversations, listening to and learning from colleagues is important

Performance Note

- Level 2 is a big step up structurally and professionally. People are confident in their place and contributions so no single person dominates and there is a shared leadership based on good levels of trust.
- Common meeting rules across the school are observed and teams often join together to share information.
- There is no invitation issued to attend the meetings. Specialists and support staff attend as a matter of course because their skills and input are sought.
- While planning (what to teach) is certainly respected, there is a strong focus on pedagogical effectiveness (how we are teaching). This openness may involve team teaching, colleague observation and the use of specialists in the room.
- There is a much greater level of consistency and effectiveness across teams.

3rd Level – The ideal level	School Strengths	School Opportunities	My role

- As above in 2nd Level with an emphasis on the individualisation of student instruction using data to discern the best approach
- The individual team gathers regularly to collectively understand the impact of their teaching approaches
- The Leadership Team is closely involved in the team's work either by being present or through actively following through on issues and through the provision of strategic support
- Evidenced based decision making, the effective use of data, the celebration of success and shared leadership is evident

Performance Note

- Level 3 is not such a big step up from Level 2 because the underlying strength of the school's culture can be built on.
- Level 3 does require additional individual and team commitment to a continuous self reflective stance and a clearer understanding of the use of different data sources to gauge effectiveness. This comes with a willingness to change practice, experiment and request assistance. Any change is not seen as a personal failure.
- Student impact is the measure of success for Level 3 teams.

Next level teams

In high performing schools working in teams is a given.

Collaborative teams are the ideal vehicle to build on the school's mission and vision statements. There is a defined and agreed collective purpose at play in any well organised and well led school. The central document is the school's Mission Statement supported by associated documentation around vision, goals, targets and any system imperatives. Teams generate better productivity and innovation from joint effort where the goals are known, agreed and reviewed. The inability to work interdependently is the mortal enemy of those who confront complex tasks in their daily work (Patterson, in DuFour et al., 2016, p75).

What type of school is yours?

Flanagan et al. (2016, p4) point out that in conventional schools two types of interpersonal engagement dominate: coordination and collegiality. Well organised schools show high levels of coordination and people know what they have responsibility for and when it is due. Collegiality is present as well and observed in people's friendly attitude, the level of goodwill and their respect for each other. There is nothing wrong with this. Indeed, it is a prerequisite for something more.

Like Flanangan, Ezard (2015, p73) cautions us not to mistake coordination with collaboration. Collaboration is more than sharing knowledge. It is the creation of something more. Collaboration is definitely a level up. Ezard uses a Collaboration Continuum to demonstrate different levels of staff interaction:

Collective capacity	High levels of teacher learning and regular feedback to each other. Skill building evolves and transforms the work of the team.
Co Creation	The team works together to create better ways of doing things that result in more effective student achievement.
Cooperation	Knowledge and information is shared. Work tasks are divided up so time is used more effectively.
Coordination	Information is disseminated and discussed for coordination and management purposes. Interaction is about smooth processes and organisational issues.
Coexistence	Members inhabit the same space. Little or no interaction beyond the basic civilities of life (2015, p72).

The lone operator answering only to the principal and acting in their own best interests is a dying breed. We are required to work together in teams which brings into play all the interesting dynamics of human interaction. Individuals bring to the team the full range of human emotions, dispositions and frailties. They also bring the full range of competencies, strengths and virtues.

A preferred state

The ideal preferred state is a collaborative culture. A collaborative culture requires individual members to 'see' themselves as part of the group. In such cultures individuals display a strong self reflective stance, a willingness to change and an ability to not personalise issues. Members don't hold expert, unchangeable positions and they freely admit any shortcomings. They can negotiate, compromise and move on easily without holding grudges. Ezard would call this collective capacity (2017, p120).

Individuals in collaborative teams have a strong and accurate sense of self. They know they can teach effectively. They know their strengths and the strengths of others. They can acknowledge their mistakes and use this as a learning opportunity to grow and improve.

This is an interesting mix of being quite humble yet quietly confident in their abilities. Another strand of the literature speaks of 'High Will / High Skill' teachers when using a four quadrant model to describe the range of aptitudes and abilities in the workforce. The direct opposite being 'Low Will / Low Skill' teachers. In high performing collaborative teams the skill set includes more than teaching or pedagogical skills. Just as important are interpersonal, people skills.

The collaborative team is held together by a distinguishing set of values, common challenges, good working relationships and agreed practices. These agreed practices are in writing in the form of team norms or behaviour codes. Such teams are professional by nature and focused on learning.

> Effective teams use evidence to test their effectiveness. If the evidence is not there, they know to refocus and review their pedagogy and approach.

Professional learning teams

A group of teachers is not necessarily a professional community just because they meet regularly. They become a stronger team when they commit to working together in ways that will challenge and improve each other's teaching practices. A school professional community is cultural, a way of doing things. It is not an extra thing teachers do on top of planning. It is ingrained in the way teachers' work together and very different from the traditional model of schools where teachers might have been isolated in single classrooms and left to their own devices.

DuFour et al. provide 10 tips for building a collaborative culture through high performing teams.

1. Create meaningful teams
2. Make time for collaboration
3. Develop widespread leadership
4. Make decisions based on evidence
5. Build the capacity of the team by providing the team with essential tools
6. Continually assess the progress of teams
7. Lead by example
8. Provide for cross team collaboration
9. Expand the knowledge base available to teams
10. Celebrate teams (2016, p83)

The greatest failures can be seen in the inability to commit to meeting regularly, attending unprepared, not engaging and offering opinions without evidence.

From the 10 tips, the greatest success comes where solid teacher leaders ably contribute to the conversations keeping matters on track. These teams are tightly focused on student learning progress and the school's goals. They look beyond themselves, connecting across the school to ensure continuity.

Using the graphic

The Episode graphic presents three levels of team. At each level all the trappings of schools remain in place - teachers, students, parents, classrooms, principals, technology and so on but the feel, the spirit and the way 'things are done' is very different in Level 3 compared to Level 1. The performance notes help to define this.

There will be particular strengths to note in every school situation. There might be an emphasis on creating meeting norms or the way the different support staff engage with classroom teachers. It is important to recognise these strengths. There will also be opportunities for growth to note.

The gap between Level 1 and 2 is significant. The gap between Level 2 and 3 is less significant because the right basics are in place and the culture is trending to an ever better place. At level 3 there is a different tone and synergy in the group. There is an energy that supports deep thinking which is not afraid of failure.

Individual reflection

- Can you nominate at least three ways you might strengthen your own contributions to the team?
- How do you find common ground with a well meaning colleague who holds a different philosophy of learning to yours?

👥 Staff discussion

- What opportunities is the school missing by not improving the performance of the teams?
- In what ways can the school improve the structure of team meetings?
- How can we improve the focus of our team meetings so we are more aware of the importance of evidence (data) and better student results?
- How have our norms assisted us to operate more effectively? Can we provide examples of how we honour the norms?
- How effectively are we using the supporting teachers in the school to enhance the work of the team?

🌱 One step further

Sit in on teacher cohort meetings with a new focus. Observe the flow of the conversation in the team and reflect on:

- The content of the meeting: was it pedagogical, organisational
- The focus on student goals: better levels of achievement for the students, beliefs about student learning
- The tone and balance of the conversation: adherence to team norms, who is talking, is the listening active, the level of trust in the group, the level of collective responsibility, the challenge in the conversation
- The focus on individual students: the voice of the specialists in the room, student data (learning evidence) referred to, students are named and are treated as individuals
- The interaction between the teachers and support staff present: the support offered to each other, the warmth of the conversation, was genuine concern evidenced
- The references to professional learning: existing knowledge, evidenced based practice
- The bias to action: what are the actions to be taken

EPISODE 8

Using data effectively

TITLE

Using data effectively

FOCUS

 Individual Leader

 Leadership Team

 School community

WHY READ THIS

Effective leaders and leadership teams will have an appreciation of the importance of student data because it is one way to understand student growth and the school's instructional progress.

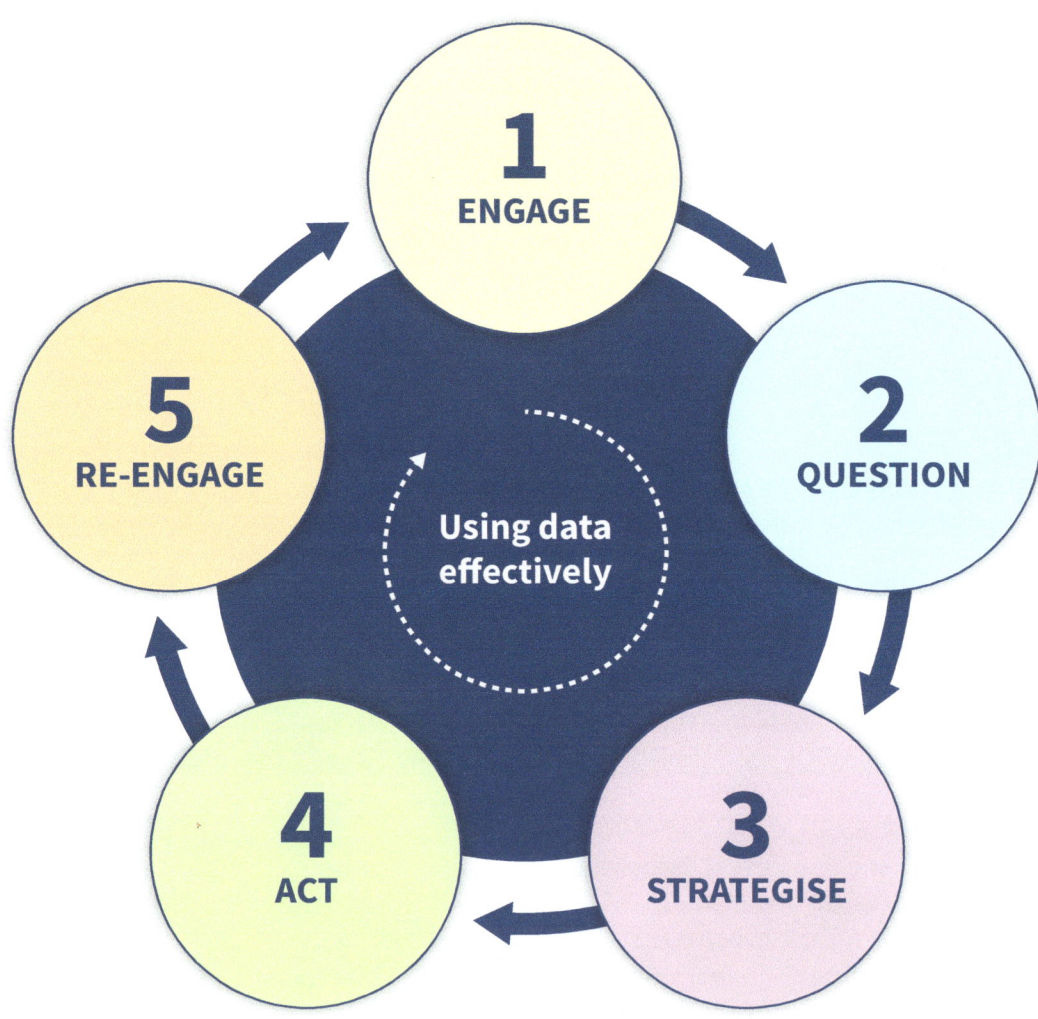

38 NEXT LEVEL SCHOOLS   SCHOOL TEAM

Using data effectively

The issues with data

There is often plenty of evidence that could be used to make learning decisions and evaluate the effectiveness of different programs adopted in schools but the exercise is fraught with problems.

There are many issues in this area including dealing with those who hold strong personal opinions on the use of testing, people who misunderstand the term data thinking it represents only numbers, those that simply don't know what to do with collected information, finding the time to discuss data can be hard, how data is stored and presented can be problematic and so on.

Data in the form of school comparisons is particularly problematic for many teachers. However, it is only one form of data presentation and use. There are many ways class and school data can be collected, stored and analysed.

Analysing data effectively is not a single person undertaking and high performing systems will be investing in building the data literacy of everyone and not just a few selected 'data experts'. An overreliance on data experts will not build overall capacity. Understanding data is best addressed through a team approach.

Why it is important

Timperley et al. suggest that genuine and disciplined inquiry is based on the use of evidence (2020, p63). Evidence gets an undeserved and bad name. The authors prefer to pair evidence with evaluative thinking (p63) because this thinking is an orientation to inquiry that disrupts the usual judgement making processes. Better performing schools are always on the lookout for evidence and impact and they seek it from a variety of sources.

These schools take the business of noticing seriously. 'Superficial engagement has been intensified by our screen culture … It may be possible that as a community we need to learn not only how to notice images but how to notice relationships, ideas, connections, patterns etc. When we achieve this noticing it provides the basis for asking deep and informed questions' (Jefferson and Anderson, 2017, p76).

Taking the time to notice, wonder and question is the secret to successs.

A synthesis of the evidential base on professional learning by Timperley et al. (2007) highlights the potential impact of professional learning communities (PLCs) as one powerful form of teacher collaboration. They note that to be most effective professional learning communities require two conditions: first, participants need to be supported to process new understandings to assess their implications for teaching; and second, the focus of the PLC must be on making a positive (measured) impact to student learning.

The last sentence is what matters, (measured) impact to student learning.

Results focus

In the broader educational literature a strong focus on improved student results and teacher collaboration is evident. To assess effectiveness in helping all students to learn, educators in a PLC focus on results – the evidence of student learning (DuFour et al., Learning by Doing, p12).

Unless their initiatives are subject to ongoing assessment based on tangible results, they represent random groping in the dark rather than purposeful improvement (p12). Teachers in a PLC community commit to using the data to make assessments on their individual impact. This is representative of a true learning community.

DuFour's mantra is Focus on Learning, Focus on Collaboration, Focus on Results. Data assists us measure the impact of the teaching.

> Members of a PLC recognise that their efforts must ultimately be assessed based on results, rather than intentions.

A team approach

Regular users of data gain confidence as the learning conversations with colleagues become sharper and the response tighter. Teacher led conversations in this format within the PLT, supported by pedagogical leadership will lead to better student outcomes. An increasing level of data sophistication will also develop with professional learning opportunities.

The cyclical learning approach is an effective way to build the data literacy skills of the team. The cycle steps through a logical process. It's not that there is a shortage of data sources and information in the form of results and scores, often it is quite the opposite. The cyclical learning approach helps to ensure all types of evidence are used effectively.

1. ENGAGE: What are we looking to achieve?

What are the issues we need to better understand? The staff will need to find clarity on what the problem is. This will also be a whole staff engagement so how is the ground prepared? It might be that there has to be a less is better approach in the selection of evidence especially when the volume of data might be overwhelming. Taking time in this step and seeking some advice is important. High performing schools make the time to engage in disciplined inquiry.

2. QUESTION: Asking the right questions takes time

It is all about questioning. The right questions to be asking might not be the first questions asked. This is where a team approach strengthens the understanding of the data through shared wisdom, quality conversation and listening to the views of others. Teams in the 'flow' understand this to be non judgemental, expansive and probing. There should be plenty of quiet time pondering and thinking. Time spent in joint analysis is time well spent.

3. STRATEGISE: What do we commit to doing? How will this be implemented? How will we know success?

When the issues are clear then the agreed plan or approach is important particularly when there is a change to structure or pedagogy. Clarity and clear expectations for everyone is important. These must be unambiguously stated, never left to chance. Productive team members provide the cognitive strength needed here. Forming a plan from the evidence requires both objective thinking and practical solutions.

4. ACT: Consistent implementation and thoroughness is important.

An action bias where changes are in full view is exciting. Too many times we implement change that really is limited and superficial only. If this is the case, why bother? The follow through on what was agreed is where the difference is seen. It is important in this stage to know if the actions are resulting in (measured) better learning. Formative and ongoing assessment techniques are always useful in testing student understanding. It's more of the evidence gathering at work.

5. RE-ENGAGE: Regroup, double check, reassess

After an agreed time a review is necessary to double check what was intended is working and is making the required difference. Evaluation is never wasted. There may be some tweaking needed to smooth out elements so that the impact matches the intentions.

The cyclical learning process with data does not have to be led by an expert. The everyday data conversations between teachers and the quality of the conversations in the Professional Learning Team meetings particularly around student progress and performance are indications of a growing sense of data informed practice.

Individual reflection

- When have you consciously 'noticed' at school? That is, stopped, really thought about what you see and feel about the learning and gathered your own evidence to support your thinking.
- How are you becoming a more confident user of data? Within the class cohort or the PLT grouping do you speak up using data and participate as an engaged colleague?

Staff conversation

- If as a staff we are overwhelmed by the amount of data available, how are we focusing on agreed whole school data sets?
- Are the teacher cohort arrangements strong and flexible enough to enable productive data conversations to flourish? What new structures might we have to consider to enable stronger data conversations amongst the cohort teams?

One step further

- Start your own private 'noticing list'. Use it as a catalyst for initial conversations with trusted others. Too many times worthy thoughts come to us and then leave our memory pushed out by the immediate and the troublesome.
- Read Selina Fisk, https://www.selenafisk.com

EPISODE 9

Strong leadership teams and the underlying vision

TITLE

Strong leadership teams

FOCUS

 Individual Leader

 Leadership Team

 School community

WHY READ THIS

It is a common enough fault to look at your leadership team and conclude there is little new learning to acquire. This is a mistake (Williams and Hierck, 2015, p21). Avoid this mistake.

Aspect	Description	The underlying vision (as an example)	Rating* 1-5
1. Open Conversations	Within the team and with the team and the staff, the conversations are life-giving, based on equality; promoting good-will and dialogue. Conversations reflect a positive, open culture.	We believe that we can achieve success in life and learning where diversity is valued, and shared wisdom contributes to decision-making.	
2. Purpose and Direction	There is a sense of purpose in the team. The team understands the value of strategic planning and joint goal setting that leads to a united direction. The team shows resilience in the face of difficulties. Celebration is encouraged.	As a learning community, we educate all to be successful, creative and informed learners; empowered to shape and enrich our world.	
3. Professional Learning Team	This leadership team learns together. Innovation and inquiry are encouraged. Members read the literature, discuss and critique their efforts based on an analysis of the literature, data and lived experience. There is a strong focus on learning and growth as professionals through collaboration.	As a learning community we are equals. We value the contributions of others and seek to grow as professionals.	
4. Relational Trust	Members of the leadership team show interpersonal respect and have personal regard for others. The team is seen as having integrity because moral and ethical principles underpin actions including an understanding of confidentiality. People are honest with each other; feedback is welcomed and there is good-will. Any internal conflict is healthy and managed.	We value integrity, we act ethically. We foster respectful relationships, advocating for and empathising with those at the margins. We are relational with a shared responsibility to educate for the common good.	

*5= Well developed

Aspect	Description	The underlying vision (as an example)	Rating* 1-5
5. Resourcing	The team demonstrates stewardship by allocating resources equitably and ensuring they are aligned to pedagogical purposes. Resourcing is seen by others as related to student outcomes and is needs based.	We embrace the future with confidence and hope. We are building a sustainable future as we ensure stewardship of resources with transparency, accountability and compliance.	
6. Pedagogical Direction	The leadership team has the confidence of the staff because there is a clear, supported and well-expressed pedagogical direction.	We strive for excellence. We grow engagement, progress, achievement and wellbeing for each student.	
7. Commitment	There is strong evidence of dedication and loyalty to each other. Unity and a drive to complete tasks successfully is a priority. It is evident that the team has a capacity for hard work.	We will see events through to a successful conclusion.	
8. Solving complex problems	Challenges and their constraints are understood. The data is respected through evidenced based decision making. Processes such as Action Research are able to be used. Serious people issues are prioritised. Performance matters are not avoided and are addressed promptly and with dignity.	Each person is a lifelong learner, with a desire to do what is right. We are all accountable for our actions.	
9. Care for others	The wellbeing of students and their families is at the centre of the school's deliberations. Better student outcomes direct all endeavours. The wellbeing of staff is evident and expressed in attitudes and behaviours that demonstrate empathy and care for all.	The team values its members and promotes wellbeing in all its forms.	
10. Leadership	Within this team the leader does not dominate. The leader is approachable, shows example, enables systems to work, is empathic and emotionally intelligent and has vision and energy. The leader uses the talents of others on the team fairly and effectively.	Every person brings their own richly diverse life journey to contribute to this community.	

*5= Well developed

Strong leadership teams

Principals who foster trust, are well respected by others, act with integrity and have solid organisational skills are highly likely to have a leadership team in place that both supports and challenges their thinking.

There are quite literally thousands of books on the principalship, principal leadership, principal impact and related titles. Almost everyone reading this publication will have completed studies in leadership in some form. There is no intention here to replicate this wisdom. While brief in explanation, the impact of a strong leadership team is long lasting. The graphic provides multiple avenues of exploration by any well intentioned leadership team.

Principals at their best

While the principal is the architect of the learning culture of the school (Anderson and Cawsey, 2008, p45) school learning leadership is never just about the principal. The principal as the heroic figure, the font of all knowledge is unrealistic (Anderson and Cawsey, 2008, p47).

A principal who fully involves the leadership team in collaborative decision making, invests in the leadership team's professional development, truly values diversity of opinion and is not afraid of others on staff standing up in the public sphere, will surely be better off than someone who leads alone and with the weight of the world on their shoulders.

A group of people or a leadership group

Collaborative leadership cultures are held together by a set of values, common challenges, good working relationships and agreed practices. There are some distinctive differences between a leadership team and a team of leaders. Kirtman uses the term 'working group' to contrast the differences.

Working group	Leadership team
Have a strong clearly focused leader	Have shared leadership roles
Have individual accountability	Value individual and mutual accountability
Have a purpose that is the same as the broader organisational mission	Have a specific team purpose that the team itself delivers
Produce individual work and products	Produce collective work and products
Hold efficient meetings	Have open ended discussion and encourage active problem solving
Effectiveness measured indirectly by their influence on others (such as the financial performance of a business)	Performance measured directly by assessing collective work and products
Processes for accomplishing goals are discussion, decision and delegation	Processes for accomplishing goals are discussion, decision and the actual sharing of work (2013, p35).

Leadership teams do not work independently but interdependently. They rely on collective commitments, collective engagement and collective responsibility. Such teams own what they decide (Williams and Hierck, 2015, p21).

Leadership teams at their best

In this Episode there are ten identified features of strong leadership teams. The ten features are not to be considered as separates that you can mix and match. This is not fast fashion. They are intended to be taken together and become a noticeable way of working.

The Leadership Team leads by example. What is seen by the rest of the school is more powerful than what might be said by any one member. Schools that want professional learning teams will never know the benefits of such if the leadership team is fractured, underutilised, hiding in plain sight or dominated by the few big voices.

If even one member of the Leadership Team holds sway over elements of the community, holds a concealed grudge, acts in a historically negative or difficult manner or seeks attention over others, then there is every chance others will see some imagined value in acting the same way.

If the school functions as a true learning community underpinned by a belief that, no matter how well or how poorly the school is performing, improvement is always possible then there is a greater chance of success. When this occurs you will hear the school leadership team clearly articulating their belief that this improvement is everyone's responsibility.

What the evidence says

Research has long revealed the powerful impact that school leadership teams can have in improving the quality of teaching and learning. More recent research is naming the precise evidence-based practices that add the most value to learning growth and which should be the focus of the school's leadership. There is now more precise language around this which is seen in comments such as: *Effective leaders create cultures of high expectations, provide clarity about what teachers are to teach and students are to learn, establish strong professional learning communities and lead ongoing efforts to improve teaching practices* (NSIT, ACER, 2012, Introductory Comments).

Writing in The Weekend Australian (Aim to Create Accountability via Compassion, March 04 05, 2023, p48) Davey sets out six conditions for creating an effective team without using fear tactics. This comes from a pure business perspective and while the full text language has a different tone to educational language a number of points are worth noting including expectations, psychological safety and coaching.

- Set clear expectations
- Foster accountability through clear expectations. Do not fail to answer the who, what and where questions
- Maintain attention
- Add processes and tools to maintain everyone's focus on progress
- Create psychological safety
- Allow space for employees to share their struggles. Avoid coming to people's rescue as that erodes trust
- Be a coach, not a micromanager
- Guide their attention rather than dictating how they will work
- Use appropriate consequences
- Use consequences carefully as a fundamental part of learning
- When all else fails, allow for a graceful exit
- Acknowledged as counter intuitive but sometimes the kindest thing you can do is to let someone go.

Using the graphic

The features of strong leadership teams are outlined in the graphic. The headings are drawn from the expansive literature base and represent neither a complete or exhaustive list. Use this as a self reflective team tool and perhaps change the rating column to one where the evidence might be listed. Additionally, the underlying vision is inserted only as a guide. There is power in creating your own underlying vision.

In this area of study there are many avenues, disciplines and competing philosophies. It can be confusing so a simple list of ten might be of assistance.

All the more so when most of us reading this are in schools and have known in our time good, poor and indifferent leadership.

 Individual reflection

- How has any one of the ten Aspects in the list changed for you over time?
- In your own leadership what three features are you most comfortable with and conversely, what three features might you wish to think more deeply about?

 Staff conversation

- In what ways does a strong leadership team set the example for other teams within the school?
- How is the culture of the school represented in the culture of the leadership team?

 One step further

- Ask the leadership team to work together to create their own underlying vision from the school's existing vision and mission statements.
- Use the school's system consultancy (or an outside consultant) to work with your leadership team based on the identified aspects. Identify three areas where there needs to be a degree of change.

EPISODE 10

Hope is a strategy

TITLE

Hope is a Strategy

FOCUS

 Individual Leader

 Leadership Team

 School community

WHY READ THIS

'Men build too many walls and not enough bridges' (Joseph Forte Newton)
If you want to build some bridges start here.

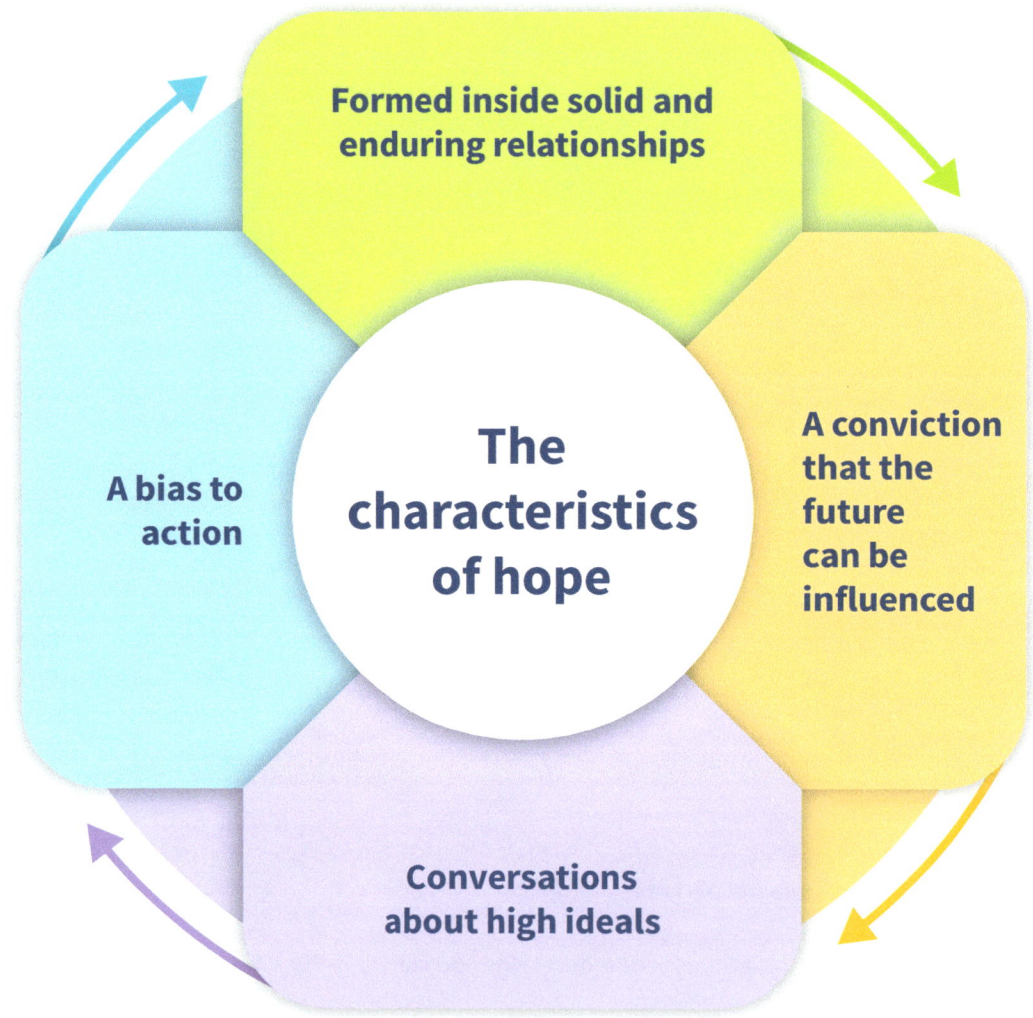

Adapted from Bezzina (2018) and Ludema (1997)

Hope is a strategy

A commonly heard, confidently stated statement is that 'hope is not a strategy', however, in certain conditions HOPE can be a very effective strategy.

Hope is definitely not a strategy when the predominant culture in the school is characterised by a certain listlessness and aimlessness, a failure to trust others, a lack of inquisitiveness and little drive to understand and improve the situation. In these situations, hoping for improvement is just wishful thinking.

However, in schools where there is team trust, energy and drive, inquiry with directed conversation and a desire to further improve, then hope is indeed a worthy strategy.

This episode is an extension on material drawn from Bezzina (2018, p137) who in turn quotes and references Fullan (2010) and Ludema et al. (1997).

A virtuous circle

In the finance world the benefits of 'compound interest' is extolled. In the education world a virtuous circle is similar. A virtuous circle is the holy grail of moral agency (agency being any action or intervention that produces a particular effect). This is where people continuously build off previous success to create even higher levels of positivity and success.

The authors above point to four characteristics of hope. The language has been extended here and plotted on the circle. The effect is not linear with no end point in this pilgrimage. There is no final arrival, mission accomplished and sign off.

1. **Firstly and most importantly hope is formed inside solid and enduring professional relationships.** Exactly what constitutes professional relationships deserves further thought and is covered in part below, however, solid and enduring professional relationships suggest a degree of openness to new ideas, a robustness in conversation and a group and individual maturity that can recover from differences in opinion or clashes of style. There is a foundation of trust. Indeed, where trust is fragile or broken then hope is hard to come by. Solid professional relationships are built over time because of the substance and commitment of the people involved.

2. **It is nurtured by a conviction that the future can be influenced and that how things are right now does not necessarily have to be the way things are in the future.** This attitude promotes a forward looking, blame free and 'confident in the future' position. When a staff as a whole and the individuals within adopt this stance there is a solid positivity and a 'can do' attitude in the atmosphere. Negativity and closed minds can suck energy out of the room quickly.

3. **This is sustained by conversations about high ideals. Talking about the best the school can be, where high expectations are the norm.** There are many types of personalities to work with and different conversations to be had in staff rooms. Not all people are life-giving and some conversations are quite likely to be depressing on occasion. However, when the overall picture is painted with vibrancy and possibility rather than with negativity, then better conversations result. A positive narrative strengthens the conversation.

4. **These conversations are given shape by a bias to action where strategy and goals are moved to targeted and clearly observed actions and behaviours.** All the good talk and the fine intentions are lost when the opportunity for action presents itself and nothing happens. Inertia and failure to lift off will certainly break the circle. However, when observed in a bias to action with changed behaviours and concrete actions then it is a sight to behold.

> ...in schools where there is team trust, energy and drive... then hope is indeed a worthy strategy.

Ludema et al. and Bezzina's work on hope correlates neatly with other leadership authors and the proffered diagram developed has a compelling simplicity. This strategy of hope is entirely possible in schools where the leadership displays complementary traits such as good levels of consultation, an interest in people's wellbeing, a real interest in their work and a willingness to be flexible if needed. Each point on the virtuous circle is further extended below with questions to challenge.

SOLID AND ENDURING PROFESSIONAL RELATIONSHIPS

As the staff builds high trust relationships you move from co-existence to cooperation, to collaboration to co-creation and collective capacity (Ezard, 2017).

Browning (compellingleadership.com.au) says that the simple truth is that trusting other people encourages them to trust you, and mistrusting others makes them more likely to mistrust you. To be trusted you have to extend yourself to the community by being available, by volunteering information, by sharing your personal experiences and by making connections with their experiences and aspirations. Your behaviour earns trust.

Stephen M. R. Covey defines trust as 'confidence'. The opposite of trust, distrust, is suspicion (2008, p5). Covey goes on to say the difference is not small, it is dramatic. When you trust people you have confidence in their capabilities, their integrity, their agenda and their track record. Solid and enduring professional relations must be based on the cornerstone of trust.

In schools with solid and enduring professional relationships there are less hidden agendas and the first move from cooperation (sharing things) to collaboration (sharing ourselves) happens.

In schools with solid and enduring professional relationships the work is focused. This is not primarily social talk, it's serious business. Stephen M. R. Covey lists 13 behaviours that build trust. The 13 behaviours speak for themselves and indicate a focus on getting the job done: Talk Straight, Demonstrate Respect, Create Transparency, Right Wrongs, Show Loyalty, Deliver Results, Get Better, Confront Reality, Clarify Expectations, Practice Accountability, Listen First, Keep Commitments, Extend Trust (2008, 136-230).

- To gain trust you have to extend trust. What's this like for you?
- What can you do better to recover from a difference of opinion?
- Where there's no obvious personal connections in a new team, what do you do to build professional relationships?

A CONVICTION THAT THE FUTURE CAN BE INFLUENCED

Seen in the staff with a positive growth mindset. While they hold conviction positions on matters of educational practice they are never so fixed in their view that they cannot change. They are always looking forward with enthusiasm. These people are naturally curious. They observe keenly and constantly look to the evidence and data to back up their opinion.

Ezard (2021, p145) reflects on the question 'What would you do in your school if you were bolder?' She believes fear keeps us thinking smaller. Fear of failure, fear of how the community will react, fear of push back from teachers and students. Persons with a strong conviction that the future can be influenced have a strong sense of the moral purpose of schooling. They see learning as the priority and take a 'students first' attitude.

- In what aspects of school life do you sense some negativity?
- What are some practical changes to the way things are done in the school that you might suggest to get moving?
- Is the school's current improvement agenda tight in that it can be accurately described by all staff and is it seen about the school in different forms?
- Are you able to point to an occasion and describe the feeling when you moved out of your own comfort zone to try something new and different?
- How do you acknowledge small wins?

CONVERSATION ABOUT HIGH IDEALS

This is where we see formal agendas as well as casual conversations that talk up growth possibilities, promote student and staff excellence and stretch thinking within realistic boundaries. 'High ideals' are not necessarily deep philosophical positions of great importance surrounded by dense language which can only be accessed by a person with a high IQ. High ideals can be simple, short and understandable statements characterised by seriousness but without hubris. Covey (2008, p136) says people trust those who talk straight. In other words they are honest, they use simple language, they don't manipulate others and they call things as they are.

Expert leaders manage ideas (Anderson and Cawsey, 2008, p120). High ideals conversations are not loose or random affairs. They happen inside the agreed agenda and use a common school language. In other words, they are managed. There is a scaffold and framework around how things are done in the school to ensure all voices are heard and whatever is under consideration links to the school's plans and the system's imperatives.

This stage is where conversations move out of the head of one individual into the collective thinking. This is where change starts. One idea in one head goes nowhere. Robust conversations further shape the thinking, subtly change the original intention perhaps, but they always lead to better outcomes.

- When have you enjoyed a lifting conversation and can you describe the feeling as the idea developed and changed to better suit the circumstance?
- How were you connected to others during this interaction?
- How relevant and purposeful are some present school conversations?

A BIAS TO ACTION

The virtuous circle of hope demands action. This means that people do what they say. While a bias to action demands possible physical changes or new organisational structures, it is more about people's behaviours. After all the conversation there needs to be known and agreed action as this is where credibility lies. The opposite is too crippling to consider and where there is no action people will be far less inclined to engage a second time for a similar result.

This is all intimately tied up in the school's culture. Behaviour is observed by others. Importantly, in schools of hope, the action element is always a collective enterprise. This would rarely be the key performance indicator of a single person. Behaviour is seen in a group sense. Schools of hope are communal places and while the leadership may be inspiring, nothing of substance and endurance will eventuate when it is only the leader's behaviour in question.

Covey (2008, p176) believes delivering results supports trusting relationships. This is seen in people who get the right things done, who make things happen, who don't over promise and underdeliver and who don't make excuses for not delivering.

Goals often fail when there is no bias to action, too many actions or confusion as to what is required from whom.

- Take an existing goal from the school's current annual plan. How understandable is the intention and how easily seen are the actions?
- While high expectations are the norm, how well-formed, realistic and staged are the proposed targets?
- What evidence can you cite that the school has a bias to action?

It is sometimes intuitive to observe the reverse of the behaviours necessary to be a school where hope is a strategy. Unfortunately in school interactions the human condition often displays itself in such ways and so it is imperative to know yourself well and resist the temptations of a lower standard:

- Spin, double talk, speak half truths, use flattery
- Respect only those who offer you something in return
- Withhold information, tell certain people only
- Pretend you care, fake interest in ideas
- Take personal credit
- Sweet talk certain people
- Bad mouth others behind their back
- Fail to deliver on agreements
- Engage in busy work that ignores the real issues
- Create vague and shifting expectations so confusion reigns
- Don't take responsibility for failure, blame others
- Speak first and often
- Break commitments, violate promises, make vague commitments
- Withhold trust, snoopervise, withhold others' authority to act (Covey, 2008, p246, 247).

Solid and enduring professional relationships are the opposite of this unfortunate list. There is no need to list the opposites to each of the sad characteristics above as they are obvious to any seasoned organisational observer.

Professional relationships based on respect, trust, care, delivery and commitment are the cornerstone of schools of hope.

Individual reflection and **staff conversation** questions are contained in the commentary above.

One step further

- The sociologist JH Turner (2002, cited in Turner and Stets, 2005, p166) believes humans possess certain universal needs that drive all interactions. Two of the four he nominates are (i) the need for group inclusion and (ii) the need for trust.
- People always seek to be part of the ongoing flow of the interaction. When they feel included they experience positive emotions whereas when they feel left out they feel negative emotions. In thinking about trust, Turner says that we look for predictable behaviors, sincere representations of self and the situation and respect for others.
- Can you recall a school situation where either of these conditions was not met. What role did you play here and what might have been done differently?
- Read this book by Stephen MR Covey.

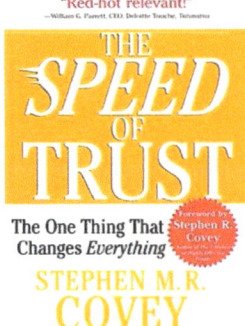

EPISODE 11

TITLE

Getting started

FOCUS

 Individual Leader

 Leadership Team

 School community

WHY READ THIS

No one disrespects the literature but sometimes there's too much of it. Read this if you're looking for where to commence the better learning conversation.

Getting started

Four ways to frame up your thinking on where to start

ONE
(Robinson et al., School Leadership and Student Outcomes, 2009)

- **Establish goals and expectations**
  Get clarity and consensus about goals
- **Resource strategically**
  Prioritise teaching goals, includes securing the right staff
- **Plan, coordinate and evaluate teaching and the curriculum**
  Direct involvement in the support and evaluation of teaching, direct oversight of the curriculum
- **Promote and participate in teacher learning and development**
  Get involved in formal and informal professional learning
- **Ensure an orderly and supportive environment**
  Inside and outside the classrooms

TWO
(Unsourced)

Effective leaders do these things well

1. Develop, coordinate and manage the teaching and learning program
2. Build vision, set the direction and gain widespread support
3. Understand peoples' needs and develop their skills and capacity
4. Reinvigorate the organisation, seek continuous improvement

THREE
(DuFour et al., Learning by Doing, 2016)

- Focus on learning
- Focus on collaboration
- Focus on results

FOUR
(The author's synthesis on the common ground between two major Australian studies on effective practices: What Works Best NSW Education Department and High Impact Teaching Strategies (HITS), Victorian Department of Education)

- Focus on developing teachers' understanding of explicit teaching
- Develop teachers' understanding of providing student feedback
- Set up structures for collaboration
- Respect and use the data to guide decision making
- Emphasise evidence based pedagogy
- Provide learners with effective differentiation

Getting started

New to a school or just wanting a fresh start? When there are countless frameworks and strategies to choose from it is difficult to know where to start.

Principals and leadership teams have at their disposal the work of hundreds of theorists and thinkers, thousands of articles and books as well as good intentioned supporting bureaucracies and systems of education with their supervisors and consultants. You've studied this at Masters level and know the authors.

Sometimes too much information can confuse rather than clarify.

Principals new to a school or those wishing to refresh the agenda are faced with basic questions such as:

- What must be properly attended to quickly as a first order priority?
- How do you understand the school and the psychological, learning and social needs of the student, teaching and parent community within a reasonable time?
- How do you separate out distractions and second order priorities?
- What works best and what shortcuts should be avoided?

Taking too much time can lead to a loss of interest in change. Moving too quickly might lead to poor decision making. Confusion can lead to inertia as the leadership struggles with the sheer weight of differing opinion within the school, system directives and well-meant advice.

What's presented here

This set of four different models or schemes presents as easy to understand overviews of the substantive issues that need to be progressed in order for the school to thrive. Each of the models cuts through the confusion to provide useful clues on where to place your energy.

These are the things good schools do well. The four models are separate, not in any particular order and one is not preferred over the other. They are simply four different and effective ways to frame up thinking so the questions above can be answered.

Common themes from the four models

Behind each model is solid theory, research and experience. Viewed together they provide an interesting pattern of contemporary thinking.

For any new principal or leadership team looking to refresh the agenda the following three common themes stand out:

1. The connection between a focus on learning and improved student results and the importance of knowing what's happening in classrooms

DuFour et al. are strong on a results focus and using evidence of student learning to extend or intervene. For these authors (and others) it is results not intentions that count (DuFour et al., Learning by Doing, p12). To do this properly a principal and leadership team need to know what is happening in classrooms so the first focus is learning. The lesson here is that principal visibility, interest in student progress and teacher pedagogy is paramount.

Robinson et al. also focus our thinking on this connection. They use the words 'direct involvement'. Direct involvement leaves little room for ambiguity.

Those who are purposefully and regularly in classrooms will better understand what is required to lift performance.

2. A focus on continuous improvement through teacher learning and capacity building

Effective principals not only value teacher professional learning BUT in Robinson et al.'s research they actively participate in the teacher learning. There is possibly nothing worse than a principal's perceived lack of interest in participating in teacher learning by being regularly absent or passively participating.

Nationally and internationally there is unequivocal evidence that the quality of the teaching is the most significant in-school factor affecting student outcomes (Australian Institute for Teaching and School Leadership, 2012,p2). Schools that access good professional learning on a planned basis and then use feedback to further strengthen the practices across the school are building capacity. They demonstrate an 'open to learning' attitude and seek to build from within.

The lesson here is that an agreed, regular and interesting pattern of staff professional learning that respects local expertise and challenges thinking is a key to early and lasting success.

3. The need to be explicit about goals, targets and expectations

This is a common theme in the literature and a good place to start any journey to excellence. Timperley et al. (Leading Professional Learning, 2020, p29) call this developing a culture of learning. Goals, targets and expectations need to be explicit and observed.

Flanagan et al. (2016, p85) reinforce the need for clarity, 'Our experience has taught us that while many factors impact success, it is essential to understand what you want to achieve, the steps required to achieve it and the ways you will monitor when you have achieved it. It is through this clarity that powerful behaviours are developed'.

The place of jointly agreed goals, targets and expectations is an undercurrent in each of the four models.

Be aware of distractions and false flags

If you are new to the school or looking to refresh the agenda here are some well trodden paths to avoid. These are where <u>not to direct</u> your energies or contemplate engagement.

Understanding this is just as important as starting off right because over the years there have been many false pedagogical starts and much wasted energy. Bezzina references Hattie's work in presenting five commonplace arguments to abandon.

Argument 1

Spending an inordinate amount of time agonising over traditional versus open plan style classroom

Spend more time worrying about what goes on in the learning spaces, what they look like, the use of the 'third teacher' and student transition between spaces rather than long battles with people over walls and doors. The argument often alienates parents, causes confusion if not very carefully staged and is expensive.

Argument 2

Over emphasising student control over learning

Bezzina reports Hattie's research points to clear scaffolds and directions for students as far more important. The NSW and Victorian research (one of the four models) is clear about explicit teaching, feedback and differentiation as consequential in learning growth. These two reports are easily available on the web and the work on explicit teaching, feedback and differentiation is enlightening.

Argument 3

Using streaming as a strategy for all your students

This is often a problem in schools and a good argument to avoid. While there might be some benefit for gifted students, the practice has overall negative equity effects. Again the NSW and Victorian research is clear about what effective differentiation is and how to hold high expectations for all students.

Argument 4

Spending time trying to match instruction to individual student learning styles

An overemphasis on personalisation through learning styles is ineffective with the (Hattie) effect size negligible.

Argument 5

Over emphasising homework and test practice

This is always an easy argument to get into and one that many people hold strong opinions on, so be careful. You can spend a lot of time here and for no good effect in primary schools in particular. There is evidence for a beneficial effect of homework in secondary schools, however, for both primary and secondary schools the rider is always on the type of homework being set by the teacher. Not all homework is equal.

(Bezzina, Authentic Learning, p55, 56)

Taken together, the four models and the five arguments to avoid will give leadership teams a strong sense of where to direct their energies.

 Individual reflection

- How do these four models match your school's current pathway to improvement? Is there a particular area in any one of them where you feel a greater emphasis will boost results?

 Staff conversation

- In what ways can the results focus be tweaked in the school?
- What do we define as our 'first order priority'? How confident are we that everyone knows and agrees on these priorities?

One step further

With the Leadership Team undertake a structured study of either or both of the publications in Model 4 (What Works Best NSW Education Department and High Impact Teaching Strategies (HITS), Victorian Department of Education). Both are Australian and easily available on the web.

In pairs take a section from the report selected. Read, review and agree on the important points in this section to tell the others about. Reference these points back to the school's experience. Why has this caught your eye? Take a sentence from the section to emphasise your point. Write this sentence up on the board for others to see.

As a whole group look at the collected sentences and discuss what you've heard and learned.

Some follow on questions might be:

- Is this our shared experience? Are we all fully agreed on this?
- What can be done from here? Are we all fully committed to this?
- How do we commence a conversation with the staff?
- What learning do we need to engage in to upskill ourselves?

EPISODE 12

TITLE

Changing things

FOCUS

- Individual Leader
- **Leadership Team**
- School community

WHY READ THIS

Nothing will stay the same for long. Stay alert and be ahead of the game.

Changing things

1. **The problem is…**

   _____

   _____

   Is there widespread agreement on this? Is the problem defined so everyone understands? Does the data support this?

2. **The extent of the problem**

   _____

   _____

   Who is involved? What's the cost? How long has it been a problem? What's been done before?

3. **What are the issues to be resolved?**

   _____

   _____

   Are there risks and damage if nothing is done? Are we all clear about the issues? Who is not in agreement?

4. **The options available to us are…**

   _____

   _____

   Have we brainstormed possibilities? How do we test these ideas? Can we trial a response? How easy is this to implement? What's the cost?

5. **The way forward is…**

   _____

   _____

   Are we all committed? When does it commence? How will we know it is working? When do we review? Is there a budget? What other supports are needed?

Changing things

A certainty about school is that change can be a problem. From the simple to the highly complex, change needs to be managed. So, how do we better cope with this certainty?

While it is true that problem solving and change management are slightly different concepts, for the purposes of this Episode they are integrated into the one.

To a certain extent educationalists can learn from business change models. The business literature sees change management as an organisational approach that aligns people and processes to achieve better outcomes. The change management literature offers many different 'stepped' models, such as Kotter's 8 Steps explored later in this Episode. Stepped models serve to ensure change is transitioned in a logical, orderly and sustainable way.

Schools can benefit from these types of linear approaches, however, as with many aspects of workplace culture there is never one complete, faultless and uniform methodology for change.

Schools are similar to businesses in that there are multiple teams operating in complex environments, there are priorities decided on by others and competing demands on time and resources. However, education's first concern should be people, specifically the students.

Change in schools can be a problem because as soon as there are two people involved you can bet there are different philosophies, fears and levels of understanding that must be accommodated.

Three essential components

In schools that manage change better there are three components in the mix - creativity, community and collaboration.

Creativity is essential given that before anything can happen in a school change process, a whole range of workable possibilities must be imagined. Any change model will not get started without a significant degree of creativity which requires people to be free to express themselves, to think outside the parameters and to wonder out loud what else might be possible. Creativity promotes a commitment to the challenge because in the end it is the people, not the model, that bring about the change.

Community is the second essential. It is within the combined group that people find meaning and purpose. The best communities are where the problem is 'ours' and not 'your' problem. Schools are wonderful places for meaning and purpose to thrive. If they choose to, people can find common ground. In this type of community, they are safe. Without a true community you have a loose collection of individuals, promoting a diverse pedagogy and operating largely as lone practitioners. Sustainable change and solving problems in a community requires the agreed, consistent, wholehearted efforts of everyone. Therefore the members of the community should not feel vulnerable (or be made to feel vulnerable) in any change process.

The third prerequisite follows on from community and takes it one step further with **collaboration**. Understanding collaboration is a central feature of this publication. True collaboration requires position and power to be levelled. It asks each individual, including the leader, to be open to the challenge and contest of ideas. Most of us imagine ourselves as collaborators but true collaboration is much harder to achieve than we might think.

True collaborators can give up or modify their position after contesting the idea. They are emotionally intelligent in that they do not seek redress in any way if their position is not accepted, they accept their own struggle to understand the other's position, they accept the good thoughts of others in the right spirit and they see the bigger picture of school improvement. Good collaborators see themselves as fallible and human. In doing so they shape the new outcome and take joy in understanding their growth in the process which may not have been easy. Good collaborators are emotionally mature people.

Collaboration within the group is essential because the notion of the single, all knowing, heroic figure directing change is not correct, sustainable or wise.

(Creativity, community and collaboration is drawn from Jefferson and Anderson, 2017)

A note about people

Timperley (2020, p62) says that in any professional learning exercise involving teachers three things are at play: (i) emotion, (ii) vulnerability (will this affect me in any way?, how will I cope?) and (iii) uncertainty (a lack of clarity of purpose). All three are definitely felt in staffrooms.

In times of change there will be emotion, vulnerability and uncertainty. If left unattended these three factors can rapidly destroy any hope of success.

Timperely refers to emotion as an 'unwelcome and troublesome guest' (2020, p45). People can express these concerns openly, through union representatives as a group or hold on to them internally. In any situation, it requires the school's leadership to dampen and dismantle their corrosive effect.

She believes it is never enough to acknowledge these factors are at play. Her belief is that as a leader you have to exert influence through recognising and acknowledging these factors and take action to reduce the perceptions of risk, decrease uncertainty and make vulnerability an acceptable, positive and important aspect to engaging in change (2020, p62).

Asking questions

No matter what process or structure is adopted to manage the change, central to success is the need to be asking good questions and adopting the right tone in doing so.

Asking questions is not as easy as it sounds. In many situations we ask questions where we already know the answer. Questioning is definitely a skill which can be further developed. Brooks and Edwards (2014, p105) have developed a list of the types of questions that can be used to thoroughly explore a situation.

Informational questions

- What's been tried so far?
- What's been the result?
- Who are the key people involved?
- Who else has information on that?
- Who else can assist us with this?
- What happened?

Reflective questions

- What do you think isn't working?
- What do you think is getting in the way?
- What do you think would happen if we were to ask the organisation to do X?
- Why do you think this strategy has been effective?
- What were the highs? What were the lows?
- What could you do?
- What difference do you think it would make if it were a different person/time/place

Affective questions

- How would we feel if the recommendation caused people to lose their jobs?

Probing questions

- What is happening here?
- Can you talk about that a little more?
- What's an example of that?

Interpretative questions

- What do you think the result would be?
- What do you think is really going on?
- How do you think others in the organisation would respond to this?
- Who do you think might not/might support this?

Challenging questions

- Why does it have to be this way?
- Why can't that be done?
- What's stopping us from X?

Connecting questions

- What would be the impact on the bottom line if we were to do X?
- How would X affect customers?
- What would X group have to do if we changed Y?
- What would be the impact on the community/environment?

Decisional questions

- What shall we do next?
- What actions are we going to take before our next meeting?
- What resources do we need?
- Who's going to talk to him/her/them?
- How can we make the problem different?

Brooks and Edwards also cite questions that shut down inquiry (generally prefacing a question with 'Why did you …' will put people on the defensive) and approaches such as bombarding or using double barrelled questions that close off inquiry.

Effective problem solving and change management starts with the skilled use of questions that respects the participants, encourages thinking and brings on honest dialogue which leads to collaboration. In this atmosphere of trust much of the corrosive effects of emotion, uncertainty and vulnerability will lessen.

Kotter's 8 Step Change Model (Leading Change, 2012 and Accelerate, 2014)

The table below is based on Kotter's model of change.

There are many models of change based on steps as part of a planned process. Kotter's 8 step model is well known and is a good example of a logical progression from exploration through to resolution. In school settings they have a degree of attractiveness because they easily fit the rhythm of school life and make sense when considering the range of both relatively simple and more complex changes that are contemplated in this environment.

Kotter's 8 Steps	Insert your problem to be solved or change process title and explanation in here (Introducing a new curriculum, changing class structures, redesigning the parental involvement in the school, working on behaviour management etc)… How will you respond to each of the Steps?
Step 1 – Create a sense of urgency Help others see the need for change so they will be convinced of the importance of acting. Consider developing a matrix of threats and opportunities. Use data to show the need.	
Step 2 – Build a guiding coalition Assemble a group with enough power to lead the change effort and encourage the group to work as a team. This team has a sense of urgency and builds momentum.	
Step 3 – Form a strategic vision and initiatives Create a vision to help direct the change effort, and develop strategies for achieving that vision. Determine the values that are central to the change. Get your language right so people understand the vision.	
Step 4 – Enlist a volunteer army (Communicating the vision for buy-in) Make sure as many as possible understand and accept the vision and the strategy. Communicate often and powerfully so it is embedded in all that you do. Address anxiety, uncertainty and any misunderstandings.	
Step 5 – Enable action by removing barriers Remove obstacles to change, change systems or structures that seriously undermine the vision, and encourage risk-taking and non-traditional ideas, activities, and actions. Watch for resistance and help people see the need for change, recognise and reward as necessary.	

Step 6 – Generate short-term wins

Plan for achievements that can easily be made visible, follow-through with those achievements and recognise and reward employees who were involved. Use short term targets so easy wins are possibly early on.

Step 7 – Sustain acceleration

Build on the change successes and stay the course. Adopt a continuous improvement strategy. Use increased credibility to change systems, structures, and policies that don't fit the vision. Hire, promote, and develop employees who can implement the vision, and finally reinvigorate the process with new projects, themes, and change agents.

Step 8 – Institute change by incorporating the change into the culture

Make the change a core part of the organisational culture. Articulate the connections between the new behaviours and organisational success, and develop the means to ensure leadership development and succession. Recognise the change coalition and those who have made contributions along the way.

Underplanned change or an inconsistent approach to managing problems will lead quickly to disaster. Models like Kotter's offer logical, considered and practical steps to avoid pitfalls and gaps. Change management and problem solving can be all consuming so success requires sufficient time is allocated with the full commitment of everyone expected.

The graphic page for this Episode provides a change model construct. Like the 8 Step model, it has a flow to it that leads from the identification to the possible solution. Use the graphic clues to explore the boundaries of the problem and begin to chart a way forward.

Individual reflection

How have you assisted others overcome any misgivings, uncertainty or anger over a proposed change?

Staff conversation

- Is there any current issue where the 8 Step model might be a useful tool for the school to consider?
- If a change is being considered, what might you say to the Leadership Team to assist them assist the staff with the change?

One step further

Timperley's thoughts on teachers and change are powerful. In your own career when has:

i.   Emotion clouded your thinking?

ii. Vulnerability meant that you felt unsure of your position and unable to cope or

iii. Uncertainty led to a lack of clarity in what you might have been trying to achieve?

Depending on your personality this might be hard to answer but give it a go. Be open with yourself about your struggle to understand, your hesitations and questions.

EPISODE 13

My contribution

TITLE

My contribution

FOCUS

 Individual Leader

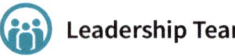 Leadership Team

 School community

WHY READ THIS

This is all about you. What a good place to start (as long as you're honest with yourself).

Things I can do

↓

Ownership
Acceptance
Responsibility

↓

Or I could

Blame
Excuse
Deny

These days demand the wisdom of the group

Does my intention and my impact line up?

Am I seeking and giving appropriate feedback to improve my performance?

Is my 'stance' in the conversation helpful and productive?

"Everyone is fighting a battle you know nothing about. Be kind. Always."
(quote, source contested)

Have I strived for **excellence** by
- ☐ Reading the meeting's papers and considering all the available options
- ☐ Trying to see the big picture and the whole organisation and not just how this affects my team/work
- ☐ Talking meaningfully to my colleagues
- ☐ Reading and attending professional learning opportunities to build my expertise

Have I acted with **integrity** by
- ☐ Sharing my knowledge and opinions openly
- ☐ Acting with good-will and right intent
- ☐ Mending any hurt or clarifying any misunderstanding as soon as possible
- ☐ Offering assistance to colleagues to share the load
- ☐ Accepting all feedback offered and not just the things I wanted to hear

Have I valued **justice** by
- ☐ Considering the least resourced
- ☐ Thinking of others first
- ☐ Showing empathy and respect
- ☐ Demonstrating trust in others

Have I demonstrated **hope** by
- ☐ Being positive, open and enthusiastic
- ☐ Keeping the conversation focus on high ideals
- ☐ Building bridges and not walls
- ☐ Adopting a bias to action

My contribution

Forget about the others for a moment. What am I bringing to the culture of the leadership team? Is my contribution to this team building community and adding value through creative and consistent input? In this leadership team am I participating in the way that is expected of every other team member in this school?

Here's the challenge: If the school leadership expects teachers to operate in professional learning or collaborative teams, sharing ideas, knowledge and resources, making decisions based on data and acting with the students' learning and wellbeing always at the centre, then surely the Leadership Team must act and be seen to act in exactly the same manner.

The place of the Leadership Team culture

The culture of the school Leadership Team is a pretty good indicator for the culture of the school as a whole.

Leadership teams have their own 'persona' or character. Others in the school will take their cues from how they see the Leadership Team operate. As Flanagan et al. say, 'Every day leaders in schools act in ways that will influence their staff's practices, motivations and attitudes' (2016, p85). The leadership team is highly scrutinised. This is the team that people look to for comfort and direction. People take confidence from a mature, present and positive Leadership Team wrapping around the school. Using contemporary language, the Leadership Team is the ultimate 'influencer'.

If I am a member of this team then I am partly responsible for its culture. My presence, actions and voice adds to or detracts from this culture.

What is my contribution to the leadership team culture? How much of a difference is there between how I see myself and how others see me?

Changing teacher meeting structures and peppering meeting protocols with a liberal use of buzz words means nothing if the philosophical, structural and organisational style of the Leadership Team is not reflective of a distributive (shared) leadership model. And the staff will know it too.

The best leadership model is distributive

In schools that have a strong learning improvement agenda there is a focus on building human and social capital. In these schools people see themselves as learners, as people who have far more strength as a collective rather than as individual teachers who might cooperate (when it suits). There is a clear focus on learning expressed through an emphasis on student growth, agreed frameworks and philosophies (like Fullan's Coherence Framework), collaborative planning and high expectations for all students and staff.

Hargreaves and Fullan (2012) propose that the group is far more powerful than the individual in school and system change. For them, the system won't change unless 'development becomes a persistent collective enterprise' (Hargreaves and Fullan, 2012, p3). In this collective endeavour, the idea of 'professional capital' is prominent. Hargreaves and Fullan (2012, p9) suggest that this movement can be defined as a move from 'power over to power with' where those best placed to improve teaching and learning are given the opportunity and the collective responsibility to do so.

Hence the vital importance of a 'power with' Leadership Team culture. This is the basis of a distributive leadership model.

The alternatives

Mind you, there are alternatives to a distributive leadership model. Many of these are poor choices or are limited in effectiveness in a society where contradiction is everywhere, change is constant, leaders are openly questioned and suspicion is rife.

Autocratic, top down and 'expert' leadership models leave little room for the genuine sharing of ideas, resources and expertise. Such models devalue people's contributions leaving little room for any creative input or shared wisdom.

A bureaucratic model of school leadership, while it might have the school risk averse and fully compliant, will not necessarily be relevant to the demands of the community or the learners. Alternatively, a charismatic leadership model might look good with that person but such leaders can fail to work with those that need regular encouragement or just a second chance or these characters move on quickly to the next job. Improvements in learning need to be sustained and long term success depends on the whole, not just parts of the school.

Anderson and Cawsey believe there have been two shifts in leadership from earlier concepts. The first is the shift from management/administration of the school to leadership of the school and the second is the shift from individualism to collectivism (2008, p15). A contemporary leadership team culture certainly calls for learning leadership through a collective approach.

The importance of collaboration

In a distributive leadership model the members of the team are engaged in a continuous collaborative exercise. Essentially a collaborative leadership style is about:

- Developing skills across the school in collaboration, critical reflection and creativity
- Developing professional learning to enable teachers to work in collaborative and interdisciplinary teams
- Supporting interdisciplinarity between teaching teams with resources and incentives.

The leadership team work with systems, communities, students and parents to help them understand what collaborative transformation can achieve within and beyond the school (Jefferson and Anderson, p156).

Robinson et al. see one of the distinguishing characteristics of leadership is that it is highly fluid in terms of influence. 'The participants in the scenario move seamlessly between exercising influence over their colleagues and being influenced by them' (2009, p67). In a truly collaborative environment this makes sense as people maintain a willingness to listen. There are no closed off behaviours.

Collaboration periods are not timed, members are not precious about titles, all items are everyone's business, responsibilities are assigned and expertise is listened to and valued.

The principal adopts a profile that allows for others to talk and offer opinion while holding a view themselves that can be changed if appropriate and is expressed as required. There is a strong professional bond in place where members feel safe, valued and free to be in the minority. 'The kind of school leadership we imagine follows the learning principles we have espoused here: namely school leadership is creative, critically reflective, communicative and collaborative' (Jefferson and Anderson, p150). Flanagan et al. add one other important 'c' word to this mix, 'School leaders can have a clear mission and vision for their school but without clarity among all the stakeholders about the right strategies and agreed implementation, very little progress can be made' (2016, p92).

The nature of the business of the Leadership Team

The business of the Leadership team is about both people (which includes the students and their families) and results. These topics are prioritised in the team's conversations. Learning and wellbeing is the school's focus and a leadership team is no different to any teacher team in that it must grow, evolve and adapt as a result of its own learning.

If the leadership team business is too heavily weighted to finance, public relations, student management or building things at the expense of learning and wellbeing, then the balance is wrong.

Teachers will quickly see any misalignment with the business of the Leadership Team. The Leadership Team simply can't say that learning is the focus and then talk only about building or budgets. Where there is a Leadership Team lack of focus, open disharmony or dispute, where the principal acts differently to what they say, where the load is not evenly shared, then there is little hope for teacher collaboration on learning growth.

Consequently the Leadership Team needs to be very aware of their own organisational health and cognisant of how others in the school community see them. Optics are important. The team needs to reinforce the school's stated priorities and must act with integrity to ensure the priorities can be met.

For example, if collaboration time is a stated focus and if that time is always after hours and there is no effort to secure time within the teaching hours, then a mismatch appears. It may not be easy to do this but it may also not be impossible. The same is true for the interest the Leadership Team takes in the development of teacher teams or the wellbeing of individuals. A Leadership Team investment would see members regularly in these teacher meetings, supporting initiatives, asking questions and providing moral and material support to the teachers.

A tool to use

So, how can I assess my contribution to this team?

An individual and then a collective self-reflective stance is a useful way to test the team's progress. Doing this formally, regularly and occasionally with outside assistance is the best way to promote a healthy Leadership Team culture.

A personal and then a group self reflection means taking ownership of the situation, accepting your role in the decision or change and then taking responsibility, particularly if things need to change. The reverse is to blame others, excuse yourself from any involvement or deny any fault or responsibility.

Doing this properly requires dialogue with honesty. This will be more than talking business. Proper dialogue assumes a mix of opinions, feelings being openly expressed and hope for the future raised. It might even include some disagreement.

If individuals are honest with themselves there are some hard internal questions to ask in this personal exploration. It is acknowledged that none of this is necessarily easy. All of us come with a full mixture of human frailties.

This resource is a simple method to check on your own attitude and contribution. It does not ask you to rate others, only to consider your own position in the team against four markers: Excellence, Integrity, Justice and Hope. A thorough examination will involve serious and honest conversation within the leadership group.

Individual reflection

- What can I do more of in meetings to facilitate a better conversation within the group?
- Who can help me check my motivations and responses? Is there a trusted other I can turn to so that a second opinion is possible?
- In recent weeks, whose voice and opinions in the school have I been listening to and thinking about? How have they exerted influence over my thinking?

Team discussion

- How can we build more creativity into our leadership team approach? What can be done to allow sufficient time for ideas to flourish?
- How can we improve the Leadership Team meeting structure and so enable more voices to be heard?
- What's our view of how others see us and what might we do to improve the view?
- How can our evaluation of the school's progress be more targeted and sharp?

One step further

Documents like appraisal reports can quickly find their way to the bottom drawer. Take your most recent appraisal report and see if the recommendations and general comments match up sufficiently to the self-marking graphic presented in this Episode. Use a highlighter to see how many times key words and phrases found in the graphic appear in actual wording. These may include:

- Thinking of others first
- Mended any hurt or clarified any misunderstanding
- Acted ethically
- Offering assistance to others to share the load
- Acted with good-will and right intent.

Why not use the graphic model regularly in your own Leadership Team (adjust if necessary to better suit your particular circumstance).

School community focus summary map

E14 Sunnyside vs Darkside schools
One way to understand what is going on in a school's culture is to examine it through a continuum of practice.

E15 Understanding the school around me
Understanding what's really going on in the workplace is essential.

E16 The enrolment challenge
The challenge of managing student enrolment and school numbers can be a vexed problem for the school community.

E17 Maintaining a high performance learning culture
A high performance (student and staff) learning culture will lead to better student outcomes in all areas of school life.

E18 Moving from planning to collaboration
One of the potentially most powerful weekly meetings occurs when teachers meet to 'plan', but how effectively is the time spent?

E19 Conversations and questions
We all like to talk but how often do we really think about the quality of our conversation. To do that we need to consider the questions we ask and the listening we do.

E20 Beyond planning
All teachers meet to plan but true collaboration goes way beyond organisation for the term ahead.

E21 Everyone has bad days
No one reading this material is a novice. We all know the drill, the process and the shape of the day. Why then does our reaction to similar events vary so much on different days?

E22 Eyes on
Where do you start when there's so much to think about in school life and so many competing priorities to consider?

E23 High Impact Classrooms
High impact classrooms are where all students learn at high levels. These classrooms have a high impact teacher at work.

E24 The learning culture
If you're new to a school as an employee, people paint a picture of the school in different ways. The best way to understand what's really going on is to observe it in action.

These Episodes are intended for conversation within the school community setting.

These Episodes are suitable for use in a team setting prior to a wider audience exposure.

The arrows indicate a complementary relationship between Episodes in this focus area.

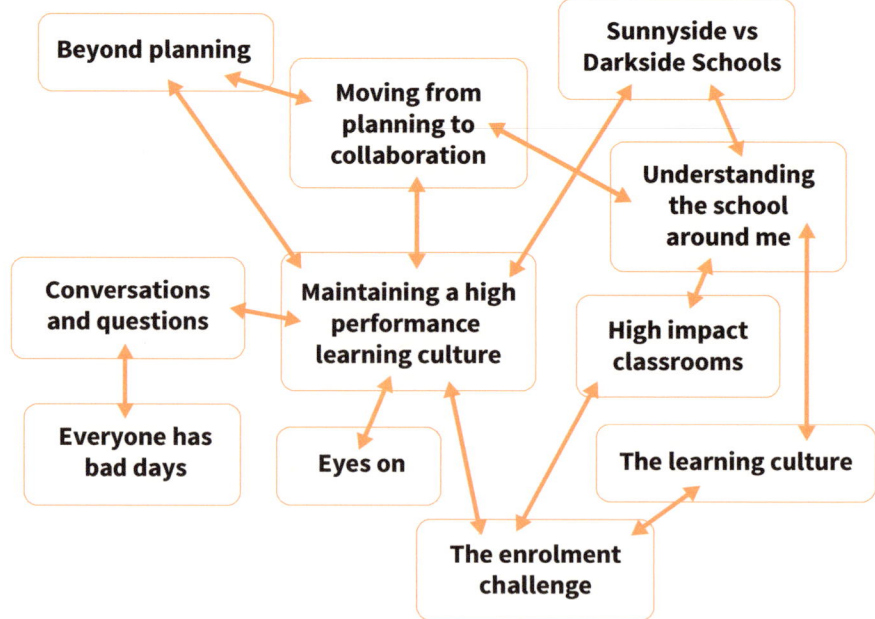

EPISODE 14

TITLE

Sunnyside Darkside

FOCUS

 Individual Leader

 Leadership Team

 School community

WHY READ THIS

Look to the extremes to see where you want to be and where you don't want to be.

Sunnyside schools vs Darkside schools

WORK SYSTEMS

- Peer to Peer Observation in place to share ideas and grow skills
- Professional learning teams meet weekly to transact the curriculum
- Learning frameworks, Australian Curriculum referenced

- Written expectations make clear roles and responsibilities for all
- Leaders will call poor behaviour

- Targeted professional learning linked to strategy and goals
- A balanced compliance regimen through trust in the staff that what is required is evidenced
- Data sources respected, integrated and responded to
- Established walk throughs in place demonstrating high visibility

SUNNYSIDE SUNNYSIDE

Improving student results + robust internal systems + connected classrooms = **IMPROVING CULTURE**

- Internal accountability accepted
- Consistent practices in classrooms lead to less variability
- Open to Learning attitudes evident in staff questioning of where to next
- Student first focus where the emphasis is on growth and well being

- Energetic positive leadership that respects professional relationships

- Parent relationship is strong, community partnerships in place, shared decision making
- Capacity building attitude demonstrates a growth mindset
- Accountability for student progress rests with the teacher, not the student

PEOPLE FOCUS

CULTURE

- High trust levels
- Strong professional relationships
- Inquiry and questioning promoted
- High expectations
- Transparent decision making
- Innovation
- Ownership

Sunnyside Schools vs Darkside Schools

WORK SYSTEMS

- Individual teachers in individual rooms with no sharing of pedagogy
- Little team work apart from time to 'plan'
- Unused frameworks, no syllabus references, reliance on old units of work

- No clear expectations of what is expected of a teacher means many get away with doing a minimal amount
- Leaders will not call poor behaviour

- Ad hoc professional learning not linked to school goals or data gaps
- Verification required because there is no trust
- Data not respected, no data systems, no analysis of student progress
- Low leadership class visibility, busy in the office area

DARK SIDE / DARK SIDE

Declining student results + lax internal systems + isolated classrooms = **DETERIORATING CULTURE**

- External accountability through formal processes in place
- Inconsistent classroom practices leading to big variations in effectiveness and parent dissatisfaction
- Staff happily self-satisfied in current state, why change when it works?

- Closed and isolated leadership using command and control to exercise authority

- Parents kept away. No real partnership only used as fundraising as required
- Teacher first focus where the question is how does this affect me and my rights
- No accountability for teacher pedagogical performance

PEOPLE SYSTEMS

CULTURE

- Little trust evident
- Poor professional relationships
- No inquiry, no wondering why
- Expectations unclear
- Hidden decision-making processes
- Little by way of new
- Blame, shame, deny

Sunnyside Schools vs Darkside Schools

One way to understand what is going on in a school's culture is to examine it through a continuum of practice. The Episode graphic helps to visually represent the complex web of relationships, structures and accountabilities in any school.

The two graphics present a broad spectrum analysis of school culture as observed through (i) internal work systems and (ii) the focus on people and the school's leadership and people systems. Sunnyside and Darkside schools use the same markers. They are just at either end of the spectrum.

In the centre of Sunnyside is the equation:

Improving culture = Improving student results + robust internal systems + connected classrooms

In the centre of Darkside is the equation:

Deteriorating culture = Declining student results + lax internal systems + isolated classrooms

The graphics are cut in half with the top section concentrating on work systems and the lower section focusing on the people. A sidebar cuts across both halves and draws attention to important cultural markers.

Sunnyside

In Sunnyside, you will see an emphasis on professional learning, the use of teams in the school, data used to guide decisions, agreed frameworks in place and the curriculum respected as the lead document. There are written and agreed norms, expectations and responsibilities that bring clarity along with a balanced compliance and accountability process. Importantly in these schools there is a willingness to learn from each other in practical ways such as peer-to-peer observation. You will find internal accountability systems that are fit for purpose, known, agreed to and well used.

The lower section focuses on people. Without the support of the people, the systems will simply not work. In Sunnyside energetic and positive leadership builds positive working relationships. Flowing from this are high levels of trust, empathy and compassion. There is a student first emphasis in these schools where growth and wellbeing dominate. An understanding of and commitment to student wellbeing is central to the improving school.

The people in these schools understand the concept of internal accountability and that learning growth is everyone's responsibility. Leadership does much less 'checking' in such environments because the staff know they are valued and trusted. People are freer to admit mistakes, monitor their performance and fix what needs attention. There is no 'student blaming' for less than expected results. This extends to the parent community where the relationship is one of partnership and openness. Many decisions are shared and the community is visible in the school. Overall the people focus in these communities signals learning for all.

Darkside

The equation is reversed in Darkside, an overall negative picture.

The people in these situations might actually be self satisfied to a degree if local enrolment demand means available places are always taken. In a strange way this might be seen as a good school as a result. The reverse is probably more common as families leave due to persistent dissatisfaction. While there may be protocols, processes and frameworks in place, in Darkside schools there is a general lack of respect for these and negativity towards being told how to do things. People prefer to meet professionally on their own terms and not in any organised structure. The same applies to professional learning where any activity is on their terms and not linked to the school goals or identified data gaps. Consequently leadership team checking and verification of data and student performance can become more strident and regular.

The focus of any change in such schools often centres on the impact on the adults as opposed to the students. The big question for such people is always, how does this affect me and my rights? Accountability for student results rests with the students and there is a lack of interest as to why student results are poor compared to other schools. Individually there will be some strong teachers in these schools and quite obvious parental preferences as a result. Inconsistent classroom practices are the norm with teachers showing little desire to learn from each other.

Cultural note

The key determinant which cuts across both halves and intrinsically linked to both are the cultural markers. Culture and school leadership are difficult to separate. Culture has to be managed.

'Every school has its own culture, even those schools that share aspects of culture derived from a centralised system of governance and management. Leaders manage culture and if they don't, the culture manages them. Leaders understand that any change will change the culture and that cultures have a natural resistance to change' (Anderson and Cawsey, 2008, p57). If the culture is not managed carefully and deliberately and nurtured over time then there will be an atmosphere of suspicion, fear and poor relationships based on a lack of trust.

Positive leadership demonstrates high levels of trust enabling strong and enduring professional relationships. High expectations of both students and staff are evident. There is an inquiry mindset where questioning is not used to expose incompetence or misconduct but to genuinely test whether one approach is stronger than another. People take ownership and responsibility for student results, for student behaviour (and their own) and of the school's community perception.

A leader's willingness and ability to 'call poor behaviour' is a key factor in where a school is positioned and ultimately a cultural marker for the school. The leader's relational ability, conversational style, conflict management techniques and professional skill in interpreting issues are all elements of their leadership style. Robinson et al. (2016, p23) focus on when leaders allow issues to go unresolved for too long. Total avoidance, fence sitting, indirectness or leniency can be used to avoid or downplay their real and often publicly unspoken concerns about teachers' performance.

A leader who fails to appropriately recognise, evaluate, confront and persist with acting on their private convictions about someone's inadequate performance means the school cannot move forward. The flow on effect of inaction can be seriously destabilising in an educational community as others either follow the poor example or just give up hope that anything will change.

Mind the gap

There can be significant gaps between Sunnyside and Darkside schools and many graduations in between. By deliberately using extremes (although not so far as to be beyond the realm of possible) the reader can see the ideal state and the 'not so ideal' state. Nothing in the description should come as a surprise because these are often a condition of schools.

A recognised ambiguity

Moving from the negative state to the positive state is a longer term challenge. Timperley et al. believe that overnight success cannot be expected as the process of change is incremental (2020, p75). Things might go well for a period and then revert back to the previous state, staff move on, leadership changes affect progress or the energy shifts to other enterprises. These factors are largely unavoidable and a consequence of working in complex systems.

A recognised ambiguity in this Episode is the occasion where you have a school displaying many Sunnyside characteristics but experiencing slow student learning growth or declining enrolments. This does happen.

A part answer to the ambiguity is to remain consistent (stay the course, look at the evidence), act smart (understanding people and their motivations) and be principled (keeping student growth at the centre). Creating coalitions of the willing, using existing in-house expertise and getting people to see other ways outside of the school experience all assist in the long term change process.

The broad spectrum approach in this model also shows a way up or out by providing the indicators for where improvements might be possible. As in the diagnosis of a medical condition, the serious problem might be clouded by other minor presenting issues.

> A leader's willingness and ability to 'call poor behaviour' is a key factor in where a school is positioned and ultimately a cultural marker for the school.

Individual reflection

- Reflect on your own leadership in the school. Where are you assisting with the growth to a more positive culture?
- In what ways is your classroom 'connected'?

 ## Staff conversation

- What can be done to improve levels of trust in the school?
- How do we demonstrate that we respect the data?
- How clear are the expectations of us in the school?

 ## One step further

- Consider your response to the vexed proposition of challenging poor teacher behaviour. Undoubtedly this one action can be taxing, contentious and problematic for many in the school and especially the principal. There is a moral dimension to the challenge. Students may well be suffering from the lack of learning rigour or wellbeing support.
- Like this Episode, there is a continuum of poor behaviour. Use the work systems and the people systems in the graphic to assist in the identification of issues and hopefully helpful lines of inquiry and conversation.
- Depending on the situation all available system support avenues need to be considered.

EPISODE 15

Understanding the school around me

TITLE

Understanding the school around me

FOCUS

 Individual Leader

 Leadership Team

 School community

WHY READ THIS

Trying to understand the complexities of a community is not easy. Getting to the heart of the matter in a timely fashion is important.

Use an 'X' to mark where you believe the school is presently positioned		Evidence space
Staff meetings and stage meetings are held regularly, operational agendas dominate (focus is on planning)	Professional Learning Community and teams operate weekly, learning / results / student progress dominate the discussion	
Cooperation among staff is evident (share things)	A collaborative culture dominates (honest about things)	
There is a tendency to look after each other (that is the adults in the school) first	The first response from teachers is focused on how any decision might affect the students and their learning or wellbeing	
The principal is the only recognisable leader, irregularly in rooms, a problem solver, figurehead	The principal is a learner and one of many leaders, regularly and purposefully in rooms, uses an inquiry model to solve problems	
The parents are clients, kept at a safe distance, token engagement and at the school's direction	The parents are partners, they are invested in the school's progress and seek to be involved in decision making.	
Teacher feedback is rare	Teacher feedback in different forms is freely given in the spirit of learning more about oneself	
Any professional learning is seen as an event	Professional learning is constant, relevant and in different formats	
Student behaviour defines 'good school'	Student growth defines 'good school'	
Powerful individuals dominate	Decisions are made on agreed authority at various levels	
The system is the foe, an easy target for disaffected teachers and leaders	The system is a partner in the learning progress of the school	
Power over	Power with	
Talk is mostly social	Talk is social but relationships form the goodwill to go beyond light conversation	

Understanding the school around me

The ancient proverb about not seeing the wood for the trees has meaning for us today. Stuck in the middle of busy, complex schooling situations often places leaders in situations where it is considered just as negative to be someone who makes decisions without paying attention to the details, as someone who overly focuses on the details and fails to see the big picture. Understanding what's really going on in the workplace is essential.

This Episode's graphic image presents a set of common markers in schools which individually and collectively tell a vastly different story if marked on the left or marked on the right. Marking a place on the continuum for each marker requires a degree of honesty but make sure it's based on evidence. Use the space to list the evidence for your decision point.

The left hand side represents a largely cooperative culture. On face value all seems more or less settled and in reasonable order. The students are well behaved, the staff appear to like each other, the principal has a presence, people share things and all the expected operational matters are in place. This might even be considered by many to be a 'good school' because the measures of success relate to student behaviour, first appearances and perhaps the state of the buildings.

The right hand side represents a quite different school. Strangely and almost counter intuitively, there might well be more robust conversations giving rise to a degree of difference. A more collaborative culture dominates here. Collaborative cultures are held together by a distinguishing set of values, jointly established challenges, robust working relationships and agreed practices. Collaborative cultures move away from 'safe' to 'honest'. Collaborative cultures are based on strong partnerships where authority is exercised at various levels in the school. The measure of success is student growth, agreed instructional practice and continuous improvement.

Why be a collaborative culture?

Collaborative cultures signal a professional community focused on learning. A group of teachers is not necessarily a professional community simply because they meet regularly. Importantly in collaborative cultures, teachers meet for more than 'planning'. They become a strong professional community when they commit to working together in agreed and focused ways that will challenge and improve each other's teaching practices. A school professional community becomes cultural; this is the way the work is done here and new members will pick up on the cultural clues quickly.

A collaborative culture is ingrained in the way teachers' work together. Such models are very different from the traditional way of many schools where teachers might be isolated in single classrooms.

Transformed educational cultures show very different emphases from non-transformed ones against similar markers. While all the trappings of schools remain in place – you will find teachers at work, students in classes, parents visiting, assisting and on support bodies, classrooms looking presentable, principals in their offices, technology everywhere and so on but the feel, the spirit and the way 'things are done' is noticeably different. Transformed cultures show in schools that are moving in a different trajectory. They are moving to the right on the table.

Hattie further supports this view by stressing the move away from 'my kingdom, leave me alone to do my work' to the basic premise that my major mission is to work collaboratively with other educators and students to collectively maximise our impact on the students (Hattie in Leading Collaborative Learning by Sharratt and Planche).

A conversational community

Community is a key element in a successful school. It is through professional dialogue within the community that we grow our capacity and develop as educators. One simple way to build capacity is through on-going quality, 'back and forth' professional conversation. As a profession we have always engaged in plenty of talking and probably never done enough listening.

Conversation is the basis of collaboration because without two-way interactions there can be no collaboration. However, DuFour and Marzano (2011, p16 & p67-68) point out a salient fact about all this talk when they say that collaboration is morally neutral. It will benefit neither students nor practitioners unless educators demonstrate the discipline to co-labor on the right work.

> Collaborative cultures are held together by a distinguishing set of values, jointly established challenges, robust working relationships and agreed practices.

The important question every district, school, and team must address is not, "Do we collaborate?" but rather, "What do we collaborate about?" It is most certainly about working hard, and while most school communities work hard, the smarter ones clarify the right work, and then work hard. Conversation about the right things, good-will and a jointly determined plan of action is the basis of successful collaboration (DuFour et al, 2016, p59). But it all starts with professional conversation.

Hargreaves and O'Connor (2018, p114-115) take a similar line of argument. Collaborative professionalism and professional collaboration are alike in that they both involve teachers talking. What distinguishes them from one another, though, is the kind of talking. In both cases, talk is always courteous and can occasionally be personal. Families are known to each other. Birthdays are remembered. Sickness and "off days" are accepted. Sometimes teachers even socialise together. At work they laugh, share ideas, resources, and problems. Collaborative professionalism goes further than this. Work talk is the real work. Difficult conversations can be had and are actively instigated where they are justified. Feedback by and to teachers is regular, respectful and honest.

'Professional conversation' is a much used yet perhaps not so well understood turn of phrase. Hargreaves and Fullan (Professional Capital, 2012, p3 & p9) distinguish between being professional (the way we act) and being a professional (a teacher). Being professional is about what you do and how you behave. It is about being impartial and upholding high standards of conduct and performance. They believe it is evidenced by not getting too personally involved with students, refraining from gossip and learning to challenge colleagues' actions without criticising them as people. The quality of the conversations we engage in as a staff, collectively and in smaller teams, will have a direct influence on our capacity. Better professional conversations mean we are all in the position of having to reconsider, explain, change or confirm our position on the topic in question.

Hargreaves and Fullan (2012) propose that the group is far more powerful than the individual in school and system change. For them, the system will not change unless 'development becomes a persistent collective enterprise' (2012, p3). In this collective endeavour, the idea of 'professional capital' is prominent. Hargreaves and Fullan (2012, p9) suggest that this movement can be defined as a move from 'power over to power with' where those best placed to improve teaching and learning are given the opportunity and the collective responsibility to do so. A common phrase is 'use the group to change the group'.

Individual reflection

Can you think about an occasion when the conversation was not amongst equals, when others (including yourself) should have spoken up but didn't, or when it was all one-way talking traffic? What was the context around this? How might it be different next time?

Staff conversation

- When have teachers used student data to question their own effectiveness? How can we do this safely?
- How would you characterise teacher meetings: As primarily content meetings, heavily focused on planning, or as gatherings of educators who purposefully focus on learning and pedagogy using disciplined inquiry?
- When teachers meet, what signs do you see of deep level inquiry between them? If they are doing this, what questions are they asking each other? How might we encourage deeper reflective practices amongst the teachers?

One step further

Consider the present community in which you work. What can you personally do to foster a greater sense of inclusion and strengthen partnerships? Take a troublesome area of the school where the teachers might not be working as collaboratively as you might wish. The reasons for this can be manyfold. Identify one or two things you might proactively engage in that positively assists the situation. Commit to doing these two or three things regularly and purposefully.

EPISODE 16

TITLE

The enrolment challenge

FOCUS

 Individual Leader

 Leadership Team

 School community

WHY READ THIS

Every school is a unique place. An unfortunate reality to school life can be the competition for student numbers. How do you sharpen your approach?

The enrolment challenge

Engagement for growth – how to engage with the community to build enrolment

Welcome
A school led system supported approach that provides for a warm and satisfying first encounter

What is the first point of contact like for a prospective family?

How welcoming, pleasant and willing to assist are the front desk staff?

How attractive and well-constructed are the school's promotional materials (including the website)?

How inclusive is the school? Is difference welcome and celebrated?

In what ways is the school a shelter for the vulnerable and disadvantaged?

How is outreach to the local indigenous community managed?

How are SWD (students with disabilities) families made to feel valued and wanted?

How are parents made aware they are joining a responsive community that will support them in the longer-term journey?

How are teachers prepared for new families coming into their classes?

How do existing students support new students?

How do existing families support new families?

How does the presence and engagement of the principal impact?

Describe new parent socialisation activities.

How does the school make the first days satisfying and promising for the family?

How are digital channels used to promote the school?

Describe the variety of school to parent communication.

Innovation
Placing value on innovation and creativity

Describe the learning pathways for students to future success.

Who is scanning future opportunities and new directions for the school?

How does the school promote teacher capacity and acknowledge teacher innovation?

How does the school ensure its buildings and learning spaces are contemporary and varied?

What connections with business and other education centres will support innovative activities?

How does the school make the most of surrounding big employers such as hospitality, hospitals and industry?

How can the school offer a full-service model of education (before/after school care, access to para-medical services etc)

Relationships
Valuing partnerships and connections

What types of community partnership are possible?

How are families encouraged to participate and contribute?

How are the school alumni used to promote the school?

Who coordinates local businesses to ensure they are part of school life?

What contacts are made to ensure local preschools are seen as pedagogical partners?

How does the school use the skills of parents to assist in creating opportunities?

Viability
Recognising that in a competitive environment retention and improving satisfaction are important

How does the school focus on student retention ensuring it is a prime consideration?

What steps are taken to address outcomes from parent surveys?

How does the school ensure parent organisations are vibrant and well used in the school?

What processes exist to identity disaffected people and what actions are taken to address the problems they face?

Are fees, charges and collection mechanisms regularly reviewed?

What outreach opportunities are taken to grow the interaction with the local community?

How might the school value and promote segmentation (perhaps a focus such as aviation, sport, agriculture)?

How does the leadership think ahead for teacher recruitment?

Do budget processes set aside enough funds to cover the exponential costs to future proof the IT network?

Performance
Always mindful that optimising student outcomes and learning growth is why we exist

How does the school continually build teacher capacity?

How is the school's vision for learning promoted?

How does the school understand academic rigour?

How does the school differentiate for all learners?

How does the local community learn of the school's performance?

How is the school embracing the digital world?

Processes
Ensuring all systems and process and parent friendly, well communicated and easily navigated

How does the school know enrolment timelines, policies and process are effective?

How confident is the school that correct SWD student enrolment procedures are observed?

How does the school check that local policy aligns to the system policy?

What mechanisms exist to ensure schools in the local area work together in a collegial and not competitive way?

Who double checks that online processes are easy to see and navigate?

How does the school know complaints are handled efficiently and effectively? Is there post complaint follow up process?

Who coordinates local media stories?

What processes exist to respond quickly to enrolment inquiries and stay in contact after initial forms are completed?

When and how are policies and procedures reviewed to assure the school they are easy to understand for parents?

Place
Knowing what the school stands for in this confusing, complex world

How does the school differentiate itself from other schools?

What events are important and celebrated?

How does the school show its history to newcomers?

How does the school express its mission to parents?

What wellbeing and learning support does the school provide parents and carers?

The enrolment challenge

The challenge of managing student enrolment and school numbers can be a vexed problem for the school community. Even schools close to each other can have noticeable differences in their circumstance shown in the clientele, the school's history, available resources and staff expertise.

The reality of declining numbers

This Episode is in the School Community Focus section because when it comes to enrolment challenges it is a whole community problem.

Understanding what is happening in and about the school is vitally important when there is a declining enrolment pattern. In such circumstances there can be a degree of frustration, a loss of morale and almost always the unhappy prospect of reduced resources. People are on edge and parents less accommodating of minor disruptions. It can be a dispiriting time for everyone.

At its worst a downward enrolment cycle leads to higher class numbers or less classes and reduced specialist support. This quickly translates to parent dissatisfaction at the prospect, expressed by some as seeking enrolment elsewhere. Community dissatisfaction is seen in social media. Perhaps the emotion is stoked by a few loud voices. It does not take long for staff unrest and job insecurity issues to take hold … And so on.

It is not easy to think clearly as a leader in such times. There are many internal and external reasons that give rise to a declining enrolment cycle. Some reasons are easily identified such as a new school opening in the area, sharp fee increases, a change in leadership when a long serving respected principal leaves, an influx of new staff, staff unrest that leaks into the public sphere, a change in the system authority's funding approach or new school processes around student support. Quite often the impact of disruptive students unsettles other students, parents complain and seek redress. Sometimes internal pressures caused by leadership changes unfortunately bring out staff grievances.

Any one or a combination of these factors is commonplace. While commonplace enough, that does not bring any comfort to those working hard to respond positively and redress the situation. Left unmanaged, these factors can spill into public view.

Whatever the cause, how do you identify the real issues, address individual concerns, give the community a sense of confidence in the future and stop the drift? What can be successfully achieved in the short term as opposed to the longer term? How do you break the cycle, build confidence in the community and start the enrolment repair?

Seven better engagement themes

If you want the story of the school to change, you have to take responsibility to change that story. People are telling stories about your school constantly. Be they right or wrong, exaggerated or correct, positive or negative, they are happening. Tell the stories you want others to hear but do so in an honest and proactive way. Talk about the challenges, the positives, the successes, the people and align the stories with the vision and mission of the school.

> *If you want the story of the school to change, you have to take responsibility to change that story.*

And this is definitely not the responsibility of one principal. There must be a staff (and parent) consensus around the problem so that everyone is on board and understands the gravity of the situation. If everyone commits then there is a greater chance of success.

The success of these seven engagement themes definitely rests with the staff's commitment. Within each of the seven engagement themes a series of questions is intended to prompt thinking and conversation. This is not a game show format where a quick response scores points. There are some weighty issues here that deserve long reflection.

Welcome: Proving a warm and satisfying first encounter

Prospective parents including those who already have older siblings in the school will be encouraged by the attitude of the key staff they meet, the physical attributes of the school and the follow up personal contact and communication that focuses on inclusivity and the promise of a positive start to school life no matter the student's circumstances. A warm and satisfying first encounter means many people reach out to new families, not just the principal.

Innovation: Placing value on innovation and creativity

An interesting contemporary learning environment that offers opportunity for a wide range of student interests will provide a stimulus for student engagement. Families seek outlets for their child's natural curiosity and growth in and out of the classroom. The local community is brought into the school and mutually satisfying partnerships result in advantages for both parties. Family circumstances these days mean before and after school care options are essential.

Viability: Recognising that retention and improving satisfaction are important

Listening to all parents and students and responding appropriately ensures the stakeholders are valued and recognised. Different forums provide parents and students the opportunity to express themselves. All efforts are made to ensure student and parental voice is acted upon. Proactive schools value and use parent involvement in the different forums to tell the story. In many ways parents are the best advocates for the school's mission and vision.

Processes: Ensuring all systems and processes are parent friendly, well communicated and easily navigated

Just because it's on the web does not mean it is understood. Clear, reasonable, quickly found and consistently followed procedures give families confidence and certainty. Reviewed and properly explained these processes offer fairness and justice. The language is inclusive, the tone fair and the follow up is timely with the explanation provided. Those with English as a second language are catered for.

Relationships: Valuing partnerships and connections

The school is truly centred on community with the clear theme being 'we are stronger together'. Multiple relationships forge a connected and vibrant organisation valuing the expertise, experience and knowledge of others. Partnerships extend into the local business and social community and other educational providers such as universities. Partnerships should promote the school's vision and mission.

Place: Knowing who we are in this confusing, complex world

The school is a peaceful place that gives a message of inclusion and welcome. The rich history of the school is told and celebrated. The school is proud of their achievements.

Performance: Always mindful that better student outcomes and learning growth is why we exist

This theme should never be understated whatever the economic circumstance of the locality. The school stands for rigour and educational excellence. Learning is valued and the school looks to improve learning for every student at every opportunity. Building the capacity in all members involves quality professional learning within a collaborative culture. Student achievement with improved learning outcomes are at the core of all efforts.

The challenge of a declining enrolment is never overcome quickly. There is often a lag in recovery to better numbers which takes skill to negotiate and patience to endure. This is a whole of community effort and never the sole responsibility of a single person. It demands an openness to change, the good will of all, consistency in approach, positive talk, appropriate public relations and a clear focus on the students' learning and wellbeing.

Individual reflection

- In my own role (as teacher, support staff, leader…) how can I contribute positively to the overall school climate?
- What are the small things I can do that could make a difference?

Staff conversation

Even if we do not have an enrolment problem, how can we ensure the seven themes bring a clearer message to the community? How can these themes further enhance our community reputation?

One step further

Whatever the current enrolment situation, start the conversation with your key stakeholders about how the seven themes can bring renewed enthusiasm for the school's story. Now is a good time to review the situation and refocus on the story.

EPISODE 17

TITLE
....
Maintaining a high performance learning culture

FOCUS
....

 Individual Leader

 Leadership Team

 School community

WHY READ THIS
....
It's relatively easy to become complacent over time. Most schools have a high opinion of themselves. Every now and then it is a useful exercise to reflect on just how focused the school is on improved student performance.

Maintaining a high performance learning culture

The critical challenge for any system or individual school

MAINTAINING A HIGH PERFORMANCE LEARNING CULTURE

1ST PILLAR	2ND PILLAR	3RD PILLAR
A strengthening collaborative culture	**Learning Leadership**	**Improved Pedagogy** (Art and science of teaching)
Learning teams established	System as friend not foe	Targeted professional learning
Peer to peer observation process	School and system goals aligned, visible, referred to and part of planning	Spread pedagogical leadership
Open classrooms (Learning Walks & Talks experienced)	People resources carefully considered, effectively deployed	Effective use of technology
Established norms and expectations	Systems in place to store, analyse and share student data for improvement	Learning environments deliberately shaped
Principal as a learner	Frameworks, guides, print resources – all align enabling clarity of purpose	Effective evidence based practices
High trust levels evident	Compliance processes that assure, ensure safety and give confidence	Formative/Summative assessments in balance
Professional dialogue promoted	Next generation leadership is fostered	Respect for, understanding of data
High expectations focus	Teacher networks are encouraged	'Student first' mindset in all staff
Aligned practices evident		Positive learning behaviours for safe and supportive environments
Sufficient time allocated to collaborate		Teachers who know content, syllabus, support documents
		Strong literacy/numeracy focus with interventions in place
		Student feedback well established

77

Maintaining a high performance learning culture

A high performance (student and staff) learning culture will lead to better student outcomes in all areas of school life.

High performance cultures monitor learning. The best accountability occurs when individuals self assess and take responsibility for changing practice to achieve better results for the students.

Measuring, analysing and acting on student learning progress through qualitative and quantitative measures leads to better student outcomes in all areas of school life. Notwithstanding other equally important considerations including student social and emotional wellbeing, this focus demonstrates a high performance school's commitment to every student's progress.

Maintaining a high performance learning culture is built off the back of three pillars:

1st pillar: A strengthening collaborative culture

Collaborative cultures are held together by a distinguishing set of values, common challenges, good working relationships and agreed practices. Collaborative cultures are professional by nature and focused on learning. A group of teachers is not necessarily a professional community simply because they meet regularly.

Teachers become a strong professional community when they commit to working together in ways that will challenge and improve each other's teaching practices. When this occurs, it becomes cultural, a way of doing things. It is not an extra thing teachers do on top of planning. It is ingrained in the way teachers' work together and very different from a traditional model of schools where teachers might have been isolated in single classrooms and left to their own devices.

There are a number of indicators for a strengthening collaborative culture in the model. When present, they reveal an interdependent staff with a strong, shared purpose that values and uses the expertise of others' through open classrooms and good dialogue. There are high levels of interpersonal trust and a maturity that comes from knowing that no one person knows everything (including yourself). People learn from each other. Watching a colleague at work, debriefing afterwards and then reviewing your own practices requires a mindset change.

In the Victorian Government publication High Impact Teaching Strategies (HITS) introduction (p4) the opening paragraph places teacher collaboration at the heart of any school success.

When teachers work together to improve their practice, students learn more. This simple yet powerful idea is at the heart of effective schools. Collaboration builds collective responsibility for constantly improving teaching practice and so student learning. The challenge for teachers and schools is to develop a shared understanding of what excellent practice looks like. While it will not look exactly the same in every classroom, there are some instructional practices that evidence suggests work well in most.

For many people acknowledging mistakes, oversights and weaknesses is difficult, particularly when they feel unsafe in the environment. Collaborative environments should be safe for everyone, allowing people the space to experiment and not feel constantly judged.

The basic team in a school is usually the year level cohort or in small schools, the staged cohort. In secondaries the basic unit can vary from the faculty to the year level itself. In either situation making time available to collaborate is essential. Time needs to be taken to establish norms and group observances, set team goals and learning targets, time to listen to others, to celebrate and time to work effectively through the agenda without rushing back to class or another meeting.

2nd pillar: Learning Leadership

Learning leadership is not about the single person called the principal. Learning leadership calls everyone to the task of improving student learning. This is another sign of a mature school. Key words in this pillar are alignment, consistency and cohesion. In these schools there are no teacher mavericks or cult personalities. Everyone's practice is aligned and while individual teacher difference is celebrated, overall there is cohesion and consistency.

> Teachers become a strong professional community when they commit to working together in ways that will challenge and improve each other's teaching practices.

The image of a school behind its white picket fence, where outsiders are regarded as suspicious and the system is treated as a foe is replaced by a school which embraces the wider relationships that are possible. These schools value the multiple interactions and the opportunities to share and learn from those in the community who support the school.

Where there is mature learning leadership you will see mutual respect and understanding between all members of the system of schools. Certainly there is a hierarchy, a bureaucracy and a central 'office' that does somewhat different work, however; to view this reality as bluntly as good/bad or easy job/hard job is completely unhelpful. Where there is learning leadership there will be respect for all workers, an understanding of community and a willingness to be part of a network or coalition. Across the system of schools, people do different work for the same ultimate purpose of maintaining a high performance culture.

In the wider system of schools effective collaboration draws on a similar skill set to what teachers foster in collaborative classrooms including:

- Group tasks established with ground rules in place
- Work as a team with different tasks assigned
- Share expertise, all contributions valued
- Few people dominate, voice is shared
- Members interact and support each other (HITS, p18).

Learning leadership fosters good pedagogical connections between schools.

Active learning leadership understands the prime place of curriculum documents, official frameworks and approved guidelines. These bring clarity and uniformity to the student's experience. High performance schools offer students experiences within the boundaries of the state's legislation.

Data is a critical foundation for high expectations and it provides teachers with information to guide and direct students as well as data to reflect on their own effectiveness (What Works Best, 2020, p20). Meaningful quantitative and qualitative data which is routinely and systematically analysed by teachers paints a picture of the individual student's progress and the cohort as a whole.

3rd pillar: Improved pedagogy

The school principal and other school leaders recognise that highly effective teaching is the key to improving student learning throughout the school. They take a strong leadership role, encouraging the use of research-based teaching practices in all classrooms to ensure that every student is engaged, challenged and learning successfully. All teachers understand and use effective teaching methods – including explicit instruction – to maximise student learning (NSIT, Domain 8, p16).

Quality, effective and evidence-based pedagogy is a key element in the school improvement journey because it links easily to other elements such as teacher feedback, modelling and leadership.

A high performance school is attuned to evidence based practice. Such schools do not chop and change, pursue every new idea or let a thousand flowers bloom. High performance schools are carefully considered and measured in their approach to pedagogy. Whatever learning strategies are promoted will be cross school, non-negotiable, carefully researched, well implemented and reviewed as necessary and there are probably not a lot of them. The National School Improvement Tool's Outstanding category requires all teachers to be committed to these quality practices.

It is also fair to say that high performance schools never stray far from a strong literacy/numeracy focus. This is not to say they are unexciting but they do respect the basic student right to become literate and numerate.

A good example of this type of approach is seen in the work of the NSW Department of Education's *What Works Best 2020 update and the* Victorian Education Department *High Impact Teaching Strategies (HITS)* documents. Not dissimilar to Hattie's work, these are the types of documents that high performance schools are reading. The HITS document has multiple references to robust, evidenced based pedagogy in Strategies 4-9. This is a strength of the document. Worked Examples, Collaborative Learning, Multiple Exposures, Questioning, Feedback and Metacognitive Strategies are all examples of evidenced based effective pedagogies.

Individual reflection

- How familiar am I with the research on evidenced based practices? When was the last time I read for myself on these practices? Am I using them in my own teaching?
- As a leader how are you ensuring the next generation of learning leadership in the school is being supported?

Staff conversation

- Nominate two areas of strength and two of potential improvement in each of this Episode's graphic for staff conversation.
- How can the school's literacy/numeracy focus be strengthened?

One step further

Find the school's last School Review (or whatever title your organisation uses for this process). Reread the report with a focus on the three pillars in this Episode. How do the recommendations from the Review line up with the headings in this Episode? Where do you see an opportunity for building off a recommendation to further strengthen the school's high performance culture?

EPISODE 18

Moving from planning to collaboration

TITLE

Moving from planning to collaboration

FOCUS

 Individual Leader

 Leadership Team

 School community

WHY READ THIS

There's a lot of resources tied up in teacher planning. Making these meetings more effective should be a priority.

Surface level view	Yes ✔	No ✔	Unsure ✔
Teachers are together	☐	☐	☐
Talking about the work	☐	☐	☐
Collegial/pleasant conversation	☐	☐	☐
All good from your point of view (or would you like a little more information?)	☐	☐	☐

Look a little deeper			
If you are observing this conversation are you hearing…	Yes ✔	No ✔	Unsure ✔
Genuine inquiry, questioning	☐	☐	☐
A focus on student learning	☐	☐	☐
Talk of pedagogy	☐	☐	☐
Mention of the role of support staff and how they can help	☐	☐	☐
Acceptance of mutual responsiblity and trust	☐	☐	☐
What the data might say	☐	☐	☐
A bias to action, plans or agreements made	☐	☐	☐

If 'yes' to the above, how are you feeling now?

Moving from planning to collaboration

One of the potentially most powerful weekly meetings occurs when teachers meet to 'plan'. It is good and proper that teachers meet to talk about the work but how effectively is the time spent?

In different formats, in every school across the country, teachers are meeting regularly to plan. 'Planning' is a heavily used term. 'Planning time' within instructional hours is widely set aside and can mean very different things in different schools. Teachers will refer to planning time as sacrosanct, personal time that is their industrial right. Some teachers will rail about leadership interference in the use of this time. It can become a difficult issue to negotiate for leaders.

Time set aside for planning has both educational and industrial implications.

Some considerations

This Episode considers what happens in those 'planning' meetings and how you can maximise the precious time spent together with a greater emphasis on the collaborative benefits. In many schools the planning time focus is more on administrative and cooperative themes such as deciding on who will prepare or deliver aspects to a unit of work.

In this explanation *cohort* refers to the teachers in a particular year level gathered together. Cohort planning is the basis of learning success and the building block of an effective school.

There are several overarching questions to consider.

1. Is this true cohort collaboration or is it just transacting the business by deciding on who'll do what in the group? This would mean the planning is mainly administrative in nature and probably not weighted to pedagogical conversations. (The <u>what</u> are we teaching rather than the <u>how</u> are we teaching it)
2. Apart from the direct cohort of teachers, who else is present and what is their role in this meeting?
3. Is the primary focus the learning growth and wellbeing of the students?
4. How is student data being used in the meeting? Are actual students identified and agreements made as to what to try next? Are relevant data sets available and is data (both qualitative and quantitative data from formative and summative assessments) a conversation centrepiece?

The answers to these questions will determine the level of collaboration going on when teachers meet.

The four questions to ask to move from planning to collaboration

This four question variation is based on the work of DuFour et al. (Learning by Doing, p59) who describe the process of getting to the right work in teacher meetings. These are four powerful questions especially when groups of teachers meet to plan for the period ahead.

DuFour believes the real issue is not just to collaborate but to collaborate on the right things. This variation of DuFour's work is intended to target the collaborative conversation on the right work.

When teachers work through the four questions they are doing so much more than 'planning'. This is precious collaborative time well spent. The theme for each question reflects the teaching and learning cycle.

> Question 1 Curriculum. The 'what' we are teaching
>
> Question 2 Pedagogy. The 'how' we are teaching.
>
> Question 3 Assessment. The 'how will we know they know' question.
>
> Question 4 Instruction. The daily practices that make the difference and bring it all together.

While there is a natural order to the questions, there is no need to be a slave to the order when meeting. It may be that at different times in the collaborative cycle teacher teams need to move backwards and forwards between questions as required.

1. **What do we want the students to know and understand?**

    This is a curriculum question that puts the focus on the lead document for any school, referencing the mandated syllabus. High performing teachers respect and know the syllabus. They are not making up content or recycling old units of work for years on end. In a sense the syllabus makes the 'what' of teaching easy to decide. This is also seen in AITSL Standard 2: Know the content and how to teach it.

Effective teachers know the syllabus. They navigate around the documents easily and reference the syllabus appropriately in the produced work. As a result they have a good understanding of where concepts fit in both the year above and below. They know how to effectively differentiate for students who may be at higher levels of understanding.

2. **How will we deliver our lessons so they know and understand?**

This is the all important pedagogy question that asks about the 'how' and not the 'what' of Question 1. A natural follow on question from 1, this question brings into play the critical aspect of student engagement and best practice teaching. It helps to make the learning purposeful which increases student (and teacher) engagement.

Best practice pedagogy is a common professional learning topic in high performing schools. Pedagogical approaches such as *Whole Part Whole* are understood and used appropriately. The use of classroom furniture, group work, together time, technology and teaching assistants are all part of potential pedagogical conversations in this question.

Teacher collaboration is vital and central to success. Proper time must be allocated for teacher collaboration. Collaboration is something that cannot be rushed at the end of a long day. DuFour et al. always make the point that if you truly value teacher collaboration time you will ensure it is provided within the day and not at the end of the day.

3. **What formative and summative assessments do we put in place so we know that they know?**

In high performing schools you will see agreed, common and well structured assessments to confirm the evidence of learning growth. Assessments vary from year to year to meet the needs of the current students. Assessment assists both students and teachers with understanding how they are progressing and where to go next. Student feedback is part of this question as is the use of formative assessment, often (unwisely) overshadowed by summative assessment.

High performing schools balance both formative and summative assessments, never overloading students. Excellent teachers see assessment as a double edged sword in that it tells as much about the students' learning as it does about the teaching effectiveness.

Any assessment is directly linked to the syllabus and to whatever learning progression / achievement statements (reporting) might be approved by the authority.

Highly Accomplished teachers use assessment to 'Develop and apply a comprehensive range of assessment strategies to diagnose learning needs, comply with curriculum requirements and support colleagues to evaluate the effectiveness of their approaches to assessment' (AITSL Standard 5).

4. **What do we do for those students who don't understand and how do we extend those students who already know it?**

This is the instructional question. The group of teachers will ensure that if additional time for certain students is required, it is provided along with a consideration of the different instructional techniques that might be required for this particular group of students.

Importantly, the students are named and their learning progression is known. There are faces on the data. Data walls are used effectively and conversations about students occur at the data wall and not just when teachers are seated. There will be students for whom the concepts are already clear to them and who need to be extended and challenged in their understanding. Lesson sequences are explored to ensure all students have challenging activities.

The importance of teacher cohorts

Highly accomplished teachers see learning as a journey and not as a set of uniform steps every student walks.

The engine room of any school is the strength of the teacher cohorts. Where each cohort of teachers is strong, that is these teachers are:

- Committed to a collaborative approach, meeting regularly with the agreed meeting norms in place
- Using evidence based practices
- Holding high expectations for every student, using student goals to continuously progress learning
- Making decisions that respects the data collected
- Taking a collective approach to student progress, learning from mistakes, observing colleagues at work

- Professional in that any differences are not blocking progress, people are respectful of others, there is good humour and laughter amongst the serious business of the day

then the school will be in a good place.

Individual reflection

- What mindset do I bring to the planning table? Am I as reflective and responsive as I think I might be?
- Who in this team can assist me with a fuller understanding of assessment?

Staff conversation

- How can we use the four critical questions to strengthen our current expectations of 'planning' time?
- Describe the ways students are extended in the school beyond doing additional work of the same nature?

One step further

It is assumed you are a leader who regularly attends teachers' meetings. That said, take a different approach to the next set of meetings and ask yourself these questions as the meeting progresses:

- Who is doing most of the talking?
- Is this meeting more focused on the administration of the unit (what is to be taught) as opposed to the pedagogy of the unit (how it is to be taught)?
- What student learning issues are being discussed?
- How often is the syllabus referenced in the gathering? Is it opened on laptops? Is it visible?
- Is there variety in the assessment tasks being considered?
- Are individual students and their learning needs being discussed?
- Can you see evidence of student data on the table?
- How is this conversation different from the same one last year?

The answers will help you assess the collaborative progress of the team and point to conversational topics you may wish to raise with them.

EPISODE 19

TITLE

Conversations and questions

FOCUS

Individual Leader

Leadership Team

School community

WHY READ THIS

Almost everything in schools is transacted at the personal level. Face to face conversations are the basis for any success. You need to get them right.

Conversations and questions

How to position yourself for a successful conversation. Remember it's often not what's said but how it's said.

Position yourself as a	Notes	Self reflection	
learner	People appreciate expertise, not so much the self proclaimed expert. The learner will use phrases such as 'Tell me more'. They ask questions to seek to understand, not to confound or prove themselves correct or superior. **The caution** You do have expertise so be careful not to be so humble as to present as not knowing anything of the issue. What you know to be true needs to be (quietly) confidently stated.	☐ Very true for me ☐ Mostly true for me ☐ Not so true for me	Two ways I can improve: i. .... ii. ....
person with something to offer	This other party is with you for a reason. Do your best to make sure the interaction offers both solace and a practical way forward. Empathy is necessary but so is meaningful assistance. **The caution** If others are involved in the solution or agreement be careful before committing them to a course of action without their knowledge.	☐ Very true for me ☐ Mostly true for me ☐ Not so true for me	Two ways I can improve: i. .... ii. ....
person interested in others	Be interested in the other person, their situation and travails and use mannerisms and gestures to encourage and comfort the other person. Invite them to express their point of view. **The caution** Maintain a suitable emotional distance to ensure objectivity.	☐ Very true for me ☐ Mostly true for me ☐ Not so true for me	Two ways I can improve: i. .... ii. ....

person with high standards	People expect leaders to hold high professional standards in respect to those who are accountable to them. If someone in the school is not acting appropriately then it must be addressed. Leaders in the public eye need to maintain a high standard of manners, dress and attention to detail. **The caution** Maintaining relationships with staff is not easy especially when complaints of substance must be addressed. Avoid being seen as superior especially if there is a power difference in this engagement.	☐ Very true for me ☐ Mostly true for me ☐ Not so true for me	Two ways I can improve: i. _____ ii. _____
person who acts in moderation	Be careful not to over promise and underdeliver. In the heat of the moment, making exaggerated statements or claiming abilities beyond what's possible will lead to further trouble. In tense situations people can rush to a quick solution or overcompensate. Always think of what's fair and reasonable given the circumstances. **The caution** Where general safety, child protection or wellbeing are concerned, act without delay. However, spending too much time in reflection on other matters will not endear you to the other party.	☐ Very true for me ☐ Mostly true for me ☐ Not so true for me	Two ways I can improve: i. _____ ii. _____
person with a bias to action	People become quickly disillusioned when there is seemingly no action after promises are made. If some specific action or a plan is jointly agreed, then follow through. **The caution** Do not be impulsive. Make sure any promise to act is able to be achieved without causing further unrest and division.	☐ Very true for me ☐ Mostly true for me ☐ Not so true for me	Two ways I can improve: i. _____ ii. _____

Conversations and questions

We all like to talk but how often do we really think about the quality of our conversation? How do we position ourselves to make the most of the conversation so we can achieve the best possible outcome? Good conversations are responsive to the context and the other person (Robinson et al. 2016, p11). This Episode is in the School Community focus area because conversations are always two way affairs. It is incumbent on everyone in the school to think about these matters and not just the leader(s).

The importance of understanding how we position ourselves

How we see ourselves and how others see us can be very different. We might see ourselves as confident and fair in our dealings with people whereas at least some of the staff might see a mixture of a domineering, defensive, indirect and inconsistent leader. These perceptions can be poles apart which is very unhelpful when the school needs consistent and stable leadership. This is the same scenario for the teacher dealing with the angry or troubled parent.

Leadership in schools is in heavy measure, relational. It is in the face to face interactions with parents, students, teachers and office colleagues that the business is done. Many times these conversations are not easy. They can present great difficulties when either party feels threatened, misunderstood, dismissed or wronged in some way. For school leaders, performance issues with teachers, parents upset with a teacher's inaction or staff opposition to a proposed change are very real and even daily occurrences.

There is also a moral challenge to many of these situations. What are you compromising when you give in, knowingly accept false assurances or fail to act when in your heart you knew you had an obligation to act? Oftentimes it is the students' learning or wellbeing that is suffering. Such human failures can haunt us for a long time.

The graphic is a challenge because self making in this type of exercise is rife with false positives. To be truly enlightened about how we position ourselves we need outside assistance from a 'trusted other', someone who is not afraid of giving a frank and objective opinion. Nevertheless, these seven pointers are key to positioning ourselves so we can obtain the best result from any type of interaction and be seen for who we truly are.

Knight's work is instructive

Jim Knight's books Better Conversations (2016) and The Reflection Guide to Better Conversations (2015) provide advice on how to enjoy better conversations. In his two publications Knight lists six beliefs and ten habits which provide a rich source of material on this most basic element of our work in schools; conversing with other people. I suspect his titles do not use the more commonly heard phrases such as 'dealing with difficult people' or 'communication strategies' on purpose, preferring to focus on the quality of the conversation.

In brief, the six beliefs are:

1. Conversation partners should be equals
2. I want to hear what others have to say
3. I believe people should have a lot of autonomy
4. I don't judge others
5. Conversation should be back and forth
6. Conversation should be life giving

Knight believes the 'habits' are the best way to imagine communication practices (The Reflection Guide to Better Conversations, p66). The ten habits of better conversations are:

1. Demonstrate empathy
2. Listen
3. Foster dialogue
4. Ask better questions
5. Make emotional connections
6. Be a witness to the good
7. Find common ground
8. Control toxic emotions
9. Redirect toxic conversations
10. Build trust

Knight is not alone in this field and there's plenty of good literature on school communication and dealing with all types of staff. This Episode is important because good communication or enjoying better conversations at school is a key to leadership success.

What's an anagram for **LISTEN?** *(answer over the page)*

More thinking on conversation in schools

Hargreaves and O'Connor's work (2018) is an example of a different but nevertheless complementary approach to Knight. These authors focus on pride and humility as two major traits in successful professional conversations. This is counter intuitive in many ways because pride can be seen as a negative personality trait. When we see excessive pride in others we can react poorly.

On face value pride and humility are opposites. Hargreaves and O'Connor take the view that pride is about acknowledging one's own expertise and not being reticent about admitting and offering that expertise. For these authors holding back on one's own expertise for reasons of politeness or due to hesitancy about causing offense by coming across as boastful or narcissistic is false humility – it withholds precious knowledge and insight from colleagues and the children they serve.

There are many aspects to our teaching and leadership that we should be justifiably proud of for good reason. Have you ever withheld opinion in conversation and why might you do this? Do you see others do this on occasion and find yourself speaking up for them?

Humility plays a role in the second part of this argument.

Again, Hargreaves and O'Connor (2018) challenge conventional thinking. Humility is about recognising that while we have important things to contribute as professionals, none of us knows everything. Genuine humility enables colleagues to pool all their ideas and insights, their own bits of imperfection and incomplete knowledge, to try to solve the mysteries of how to help the child learn and develop. It enables leaders to share and distribute their leadership, to release the knowledge and expertise possessed by others.

The hardest part for leaders is admitting that, on occasion, we do not really know what the solution might be. Too many people act like they know everything, understand everything and can solve anything. Often we need others to help us think it through. This surely is part of our professionalism. Inquiring together and acting upon the pooled knowledge is the essence of collaborative professionalism.

Hargreaves and O'Connor's work aligns with Knight's six beliefs, particularly that conversation should be back and forth and conversation partners are equals, which is suggestive that we are learning from each other during the conversation.

Using questions

Ezard (2015) believes (the right type of) questioning is a vital component in growth conversations. That would be questioning to discover, to explore, to gently press and to push the thinking; not questioning intended to destroy, pull apart, belittle or promote the questioner. Note the big difference here. And of course, it's often not what is said, but how it is said that makes the biggest difference.

Ezard prefers a style of questioning that is expansive and non-judgemental. This style creates flow which is suggestive of Knight's view that conversations should be back and forth. Some useful leading questions that promote this habit might be:

- What were the reasons behind that decision?
- What learning came out of that experience?
- Did anyone else have a different perspective on that situation? (2015, p107)

Questions that look to the future that challenge yet assume possibility and opportunity could be:

- What is the most important priority for us straight away?
- Out of all these options, which is most closely aligned to what we think would most benefit this group of students?
- How are we giving the students a voice in this decision process?
- What will we need to be mindful of as we implement this across the school?
- What does our community expect of us? (2015, p107)

SILENT

In summary

Being a good communicator requires a measure of self-reflection during and post conversation. An ability to see what is really going on during the conversation is vital. In the Death of Expertise (2019, p45), Nichols believes that the specific reason that unskilled or incompetent people overestimate their abilities far more than others is because they lack a key skill called 'metacognition'.

Metacognition is the ability to have an awareness and understanding of one's own thought processes. Another way to say this is thinking about your thinking. Metacognition is a higher order skill and particularly useful in problem solving.

Good bands know how to work the crowd; great speakers respond to the mood of the audience, top surgeons know when to change their approach; clever marketers know a great line in an advertisement. Their less competent counterparts, by comparison, miss the opportunity. They follow a particular pattern or formula all the while thinking they are doing a great job.

Individual reflection

- While we think everyone is equal, we can easily engage in top-down conversations. How do you position yourself to guard against any hierarchy imbalance?
- How do you know the opinion of the teachers on any matter of substance?
- Can you recall times when you know the other party left dissatisfied, upset or confused? What did you do to remedy the situation?
- When have you stepped back, reconsidered your position in the light of the conversation and changed course? (Metacognition)
- As a professional teacher what pedagogical skill are you particularly proud of and why? In group conversation how do you express your opinion in related matters?

Staff conversation

- In an environment where we have an agreed system improvement agenda which is tight, how do we provide for individual autonomy within a structured system response?
- How can you get the 'back and forward' conversation going better in your teacher cohort?
- We all say we try to be non-judgemental but we are judging all the time. How can we leave this very human trait and enter the conversation without a fixed mindset?
- How strong and observed are the conversational protocols in your school? Are teachers aware of the importance of protocols for meetings?
- When has the staff gone beyond the courteous, the surface level, to get to the heart of the matter? Describe a situation where you spoke both courteously and with honesty.

One step further

It is very easy to convince yourself that none of this is a problem for you. After all, you're pretty good.

Here's a few things to consider:

(i) Why not (openly) record a conversation with a colleague or ask a trusted other for advice on how well you listen.

(ii) If you have a performance appraisal coming up, be brave and ask that there is a focus on your conversation style, listening habits and questioning skills.

(iii) Take the lead graphic for this Episode and ask someone who is not necessarily a confidant or personal friend at school to answer on your behalf.

EPISODE 20

TITLE

Beyond planning

FOCUS

 Individual Leader

 Leadership Team

 School community

WHY READ THIS

Think differently about the teams in the school. Moving to a professional learning team (PLT) model is a great way to power up collaboration.

Beyond planning

Use an 'X' to mark where you believe the school is presently positioned

Teacher as sole instructor, one classroom = one teacher	Instructional leaders in the classroom working alongside teachers
'Motel' style classrooms (children in, doors closed, air conditioning on)	Flexible learning spaces, planned student movement evident
Teachers gather to plan	Teachers gather and are supported by colleagues to inquire into effectiveness and focus on student growth
Most teachers contribute, they are nice to each other	All members engage with respectful enthusiasm
Textbooks are heavily used	Variety of resources used in collaborative time but the emphasis is on interpreting and using the syllabus
Summative assessment dominates, lots of tests	Mixture of formative and summative assessment, good understanding of assessment for, of and as learning by the teachers
Little teacher accountability for student results (not my fault)	Full analysis of the pedagogical capabilities of the teacher when analysing students' academic growth
Vague promises are made to each other when planning	Explicit improvement agenda in place, visible and known to all
A teacher's pattern of behaviour and response to situations is relatively fixed	The teacher can change their behaviour and response on reflection of the evidence
If it is used, technology is a distraction or reward	Fully integrated and purposeful use of technology
The classroom reflects the teacher's personality (it's all about me)	The classroom reflects the student learning (it's all about us)
The teacher is the expert	The teacher is a learner
The teacher has a mark book, the results reflect the student's effort	The teacher uses analytical tools to measure student growth, the data reflects the effectiveness of both the teaching and the learning
Motto: I teach, they learn (or not, as the case may be)	Motto: I learn as I teach

Beyond planning

All teachers meet to plan but true collaboration goes way beyond organisation for the term ahead.

For some time now the notion of a professional learning team or community (PLT or PLC) has gathered momentum, however, there remains a degree of confusion about exactly what is a PLC. Timperley et al. (2007) believes professional learning communities (PLCs) are a powerful form of teacher collaboration. And there's a big gap between cooperation and collaboration.

For this Episode the term PLC refers to the school gathered as a whole, as one community. A Professional Learning Team (PLT) is usually a smaller unit, a cohort of teachers or a subject based group of staff.

It is relatively easy for any group of well-meaning and dedicated teachers to consider themselves as a professional learning team. You might hear it said often in schools. Ezard (2015, p73) asks us not to confuse coordination (organising things) with collaboration, the essential ingredient in any PLT. Coordination and cooperation are necessary ingredients on the continuum to a PLC but they are only part of the way to a truly collaborative community.

Timperley et al. (2007) note that before a PLT can exist two conditions must be met: (i) participants need to be supported to process new understandings and to assess their implications for teaching; and (ii) the focus of the PLC must be on making a positive (measured) impact to student learning.

Definitions

The ACER Professional Learning Community Framework (PLCF) is a useful guide for understanding schools as communities of professionals. The ACER Professional Learning Community Framework nominates five domains that mark out a PLC:

1. A professional culture
2. Leadership that fosters and supports a professional culture
3. A focus on student engagement, learning and well-being
4. A focus on improving professional knowledge and practice
5. Teachers that are thinking systematically about their practice and learning from experience (ACER, Discover, 2018).

DuFour (2004) defines a professional learning community as: '…a group of educators committed to working collaboratively in ongoing processes of collective inquiry and action research to achieve better results for the students they serve. Professional learning communities operate under the assumption that the key to improved learning for students is continuous, job embedded learning for educators.'

These definitions clearly take the concept of teachers meeting to 'plan' way beyond writing up a program of work. A PLT meets to transact the pedagogy, not as a meeting to write up a unit of work. A PLC is where teachers inquire and learn together to develop new practices that will improve learner outcomes (Harris & Jones, 2010).

Another definition of a PLC sees it as a framework of 'Professional educators working collectively and purposefully to create and sustain a culture of learning for all students and adults' (Hipp and Huffman, 2010, p12). Importantly a PLC is not a talking shop or a therapy group. Its key purpose is to engage professionals in disciplined, collaborative inquiry to generate new approaches to learning and teaching that will have a positive impact on student outcomes (Harris and Jones, 2010).

Observed in action

How might an observer of a PLT in operation judge its effectiveness:

1. Is the PLT work authentic? Are the members faithful to the concept? (Look for members' engagement, presence, contributions, ownership of the group)
2. Is the PLT work being applied at a superficial or deep level? (Look for the quality of the back and forth conversation, evidence of the use of data, the questioning of each other's views, is actual student progress being discussed, are work samples on the table, length of the meetings, the observance of norms)
3. Is there evidence of a positive impact on students/teachers at the school and system level? (Look for levels of teacher enthusiasm, teacher professional growth, the level sharing between classes and schools, improved student results)
4. Is provision in place to sustain the PLT work? (Look for the level of the principal's support, specialist teacher interactions in the meeting, when the meeting was conducted, follow up agreements reached.)

Timperley argues that engaging in rigorous inquiry into teaching and learning practices helps educators to identify the gaps between students' learning and teachers' practices that consequently lead to improved outcomes for students. This is a reference to the PLTs deep level inquiry.

The place of 'thinking' in a PLT

Ritchhard (2015, p3) in Creating Cultures of Thinking asks the question 'When and where have you been part of a culture of thinking?' This is where each person's thinking was valued, visible and actively promoted as part of the regular day to day experience of the group. In such groups you feel pushed to think and to advance your own thinking. These groups demonstrate:

1. A sense of purpose to the learning being undertaken
2. Commitment to the task at hand and to the effective functioning of the group
3. Equity where everyone is a learner, even the leader, no less than any other
4. Engagement where everyone takes part, no silent sitting back on the sidelines
5. Challenge where everyone's thinking is pushed, people question, wonder out loud
6. Connection where people can see the whole picture and not just the immediacy of the problem or conversation.

Any deep level inquiry into why a particular group of students is not progressing or figuring out how to extend those students who already know the concept, requires a degree of thinking. For Ritchhard these are the six conditions for a culture of thinking to exist.

When you're in a PLT these are the conversations that are more focused, direct and purposeful. This is way beyond the 'what' we will be teaching.

The quality of the conversation is important. The University of Missouri Inclusion, Diversity and Equity department calls this 'dialogue' and defines dialogue as:

- Rooted in democratic discussion, not in debate or argument
- Allowing participants to hear, share and consider different perspectives and personal experiences
- Providing an opportunity to discover areas of common concern (Guide to Facilitating Dialogues, diversity@missouri.edu).

Among other things, dialogue asks participants to withhold judgement, ask if in doubt, seek first to understand, listen actively and intentionally, refrain from speaking for others and keep an open mind.

Conversation in a well-functioning PLT is all these things. It is never never idle; it is insightful and considered and focused on the learning.

When a completely new group of teachers meet for the first time at the start of the year it will take time and commitment to develop into a PLT. With everyone's commitment and a developing understanding of what the intention of a PLT is and is not, and with leadership support, a PLT can be created.

A school where all teacher cohorts are endeavouring to work as a PLT will be well on the way to being a learning community. As Peter Senge wrote in the Fifth Discipline: The Art and Practice of the Learning Organisation (1990), when we embrace dialogue 'collectively, we can be more insightful, more intelligent than we can possibly be individually'.

> Professional learning communities need time and opportunities for peer review based on evidence about teaching practices, the quality of opportunities for students to learn, and student progress in learning. Activities that de-privatise practice and use feedback from colleagues and students are critical to professional learning communities, but fostering such practices depends on determined and resilient leadership.
>
> **Developing a professional learning community - ACER Discover**

 **Individual reflection**

- When were you part of a group that persevered with a learning conversation? What was the actual issue under consideration? How did you contribute to the conversation?
- How do you know when to speak up, when to listen, when to question others? What prompts you to speak, listen or question in a meeting?

👥 Staff conversation

- How can we encourage more conversation around pedagogy (the 'how' we are teaching) in our cohort meetings?
- Can we collectively identify a learning issue pertinent to this school (for example: low performance in NAPLAN, poor understanding of what 'A' constitutes, too many students absent from school, number of students failing to reach benchmarks) that the individual year levels can discuss before coming back to the whole staff? (Working on deep level inquiry)

🔥 One step further

- According to the Australian Professional Standard for Principals, a fundamental role of school principals is to, 'work with and through others to build a professional learning community that is focused on the continuous improvement of teaching and learning.'
- The difficulty, however, is that creating a professional learning community may be a significant challenge, particularly when traditional norms of privacy, territory and hierarchy prevail among a school's teaching staff. Creating a professional learning community often means challenging these norms head on and establishing new norms around what it means to be a member of an accountable professional learning community. Developing a professional learning community - ACER Discover
- How will you challenge privacy, territory and hierarchy head on and if necessary, establish new norms?
- Who will support you in this challenge?

EPISODE 21

TITLE
Everyone has bad days

FOCUS

 Individual Leader

 Leadership Team

 School community

WHY READ THIS
Understanding what's going on within yourself is always helpful.

Everyone has bad days

Situational Intensities

Movement
People
Engagement
Distractions
Task
Mood

As the Situational Intensitites relax, physiological measures* move back towards the resting state.

Resting state
Quiet time
Relaxed, calm
Untroubled

Rising state
Incidents cause the mix of the six Situational Intensities to change resulting in a fine physiological shift.

Heightened state
Further complications to the Situational Intensities compound the interaction resulting in significant physiological or psychological changes.

*Measures included blood pressure, heart rate and can be observed as sweating, blotched skin, fidgeting, lack of focus or shortness of breath, as examples.

94 **NEXT LEVEL SCHOOLS**   SCHOOL COMMUNITY

Everyone has bad days

No one reading this material is a novice. We all know the drill, the process and the shape of the day. Why then does our reaction to similar events vary so much on different days?

Many school tasks and interactions are reasonably routine and predictable. Attendance at staff meetings and planning sessions, meeting with the principal, dealing with student discipline or engaging with systemic office staff are all simply part of the job and largely unavoidable.

Other aspects of the job are possibly less routine or less welcome but nevertheless and often unfortunately, simply part of the job as well. Dealing with difficult children, in receipt of an aggressive email or being confronted by a parent or colleague (regrettably) happens to everyone.

On face value it would appear reasonably self-evident that disciplining students, arguing with supervisors or meeting funding deadlines are all examples of possible stressors giving rise to anything from mild discomfort to deep anxiety. The reality is sometimes they are, sometimes they're not.

Sometimes we love to be on our feet talking. Sometimes a deadline is the motivation to get the job done or tough talking feels good to get it off our chest. It is all quite idiosyncratic but that does not fully explain why some days are worse than others.

Looking wider at 'event reaction'

This Episode presents a model titled 'Situational Intensity' (SI). It's a fancy title but really it's just another way to view one's 'event reaction' in a school context. It puts the focus on the wider situation surrounding the event, rather than solely on the event itself. Nothing occurs in isolation in a school and when we consider the wider factors around what was going on, a fuller understanding of the reaction develops.

SI recognises that for any person the school day is in a state of constant flux. The very nature of administering or teaching places us in a state of constant interruption. We are always faced with unfinished work, unannounced visitors and unavoidable situations. While some of these might be welcome distractions, others are surely not so welcome. Some distractions might be of consequence; others might only require a nod of the head or a smile to diffuse. This is all part of the rhythm of the teaching and administering day.

In the model opposite there are six elements to understanding SI. In any interaction, any number of these elements might be in play and affecting a person's physical and emotional response. They must be regarded as neither good nor bad. They are just present but alone or together they can change the situation instantly.

The six elements

Your movement: In this situation how much physical activity was being expended before and at the time of the event. Walking, standing, sitting or rushing from one place to another are all using different energy levels. Consider this in the context of the full day as well. Was the day one of constant movement where the admirable goal of 10000 steps was surpassed, never catching your breath or was it perhaps a more sedentary office type of day? The extent of your movement in a day is important to understand. Even simple things like actually eating lunch in a seat as opposed to eating on duty can have a cumulative effect.

The people you are dealing with: Who was involved with you in the interaction; for example staff, peers, principal, parents, student(s), supervisor? Did the interaction involve more than one person? What is the nature of their professional relationship to you? Is the person routinely difficult? Was there a difference in authority levels; are you accountable to them in any way? The state of your relationships is a key factor in school life. Not everyone is easy to deal with and all of us know someone we'd prefer not to have to confront.

Your degree of engagement: Is the thinking required to process the event intense or mild in this case? Is it a demanding conversation requiring close attention and careful responses or is it a conversation where your mind wanders off? Was this interaction expected or did it happen without any foreknowledge or preparation on your part? If this is paperwork or a paper response, how much concentration is needed to respond? We all know when we are switched on with a razor sharp alertness and when we can 'play act' or feign interest. High degrees of engagement will mean a physiological response like raised blood pressure and increased heart rate.

The distractions around you: At the time are there other people or matters competing for your attention? Is this current event a welcome distraction or is it further complicating the day? Does the distraction require an urgent response from you (is this a broken bone, angry parent or is someone simply asking to swap duties)?

The task you are engaged in: Exactly what are you required to be doing at the time? Is it simple routine management or does it require a higher level of concentrated abstract thinking to achieve a solution? Is it an unusual event, different or challenging for you? Is the task something you dread (such as teacher performance management) or one that is quite enjoyable? Is negotiating or compromise involved or can the outcome be quickly reached? Do you have that sinking feeling this could get worse?

What is your mood at the time: Importantly where is your head in all this? Are you in good humour, alert, energetic and interested in people or just the opposite - feeling weary, bored, unloved or worried about your teenager? Are there partner, family or friendship matters weighing heavily on your mood at this time? Our emotional wellbeing is hugely important in the shape of the day and a big factor in how we arrive at and leave the school grounds.

SI in practice

Overlay any of these SI elements and see how they can change the complexion of the interaction.

Here's a common enough and often unpleasant scenario: Facing the angry parent. The situational intensity of this interaction could vary wildly from:

- Being well prepared with all the facts to hand, with witnesses in tow or being totally underprepared with no information or support around you (degree of engagement, the people you are dealing with)
- Being in your office area as the person enters or running to the office from yet another serious matter with your mind in many places (movement, distractions and degree of engagement)
- After the initial onslaught, easily finding a durable and agreeable solution to the not-so-easy task of negotiating a series of complex demands with their associated threats (task and degree of engagement)
- Feeling alert and energetic at the time to feeling depressed and anxious for whatever reasons even before the person arrived (mood)
- Knowing the person well and having successfully worked with them in the past to encountering a new person who clearly feels vindicated, superior and entitled (the people you are dealing with)

At its worst, this interaction is likely to be a disaster. At its best, it might be a victory for common sense, diplomacy and skillful practice.

There are countless interactions in the week, each one with its own context and intensity. No wonder school leaders go home exhausted, exhilarated, or both.

 ## Individual reflection

- How can I use the elements of Situational Intensities to better prepare for the day ahead?
- Take a recent unsuccessful interaction you've had and use the elements of Situational Intensities to better understand your response.
- Where do I fall down and need to focus more so I am better placed to respond? (This might be paying attention to detail, really listening in the first place, a better awareness of the possible implications)

 ## Staff conversation

- How well do our staff charters and agreed ways of working documents align with the elements of Situational Intensities?
- What can we reasonably do as a staff to lessen potential SI elements in the school that might cause distress?
- How do we acknowledge and accept that those with whom we come into contact are dealing with their own SI at the same time?

 ## One step further

For a quick introduction and easy read into the research behind emotional intelligence read *Emotional Intelligence 2.0* by Bradberry and Greaves (2009, TalentSmart). Emotional Intelligence is all about daily living and has four key skills: self-awareness, self-management, social awareness and relationship management. Understanding Emotional Intelligence will help with reducing the number of stressful days.

EPISODE 22

TITLE

Eyes on

FOCUS

 Individual Leader

 Leadership Team

🟠 School community

WHY READ THIS

Don't be distracted by the multitude of events and opinions around you. Keep your eyes firmly on the right things.

Eyes on

Eyes on the Teams
What you doing to ensure the different teams are working collaboratively?

Eyes on Teaching and Learning
What are you doing to ensure you know what's being taught and how the students are responding?

Eyes on outcomes and student wellbeing
What are you doing to ensure that there are visible and sustained improvements in student outcomes and wellbeing?

Eyes on

Where do you start when there's so much to think about in school life and so many competing priorities to consider? It can be confusing knowing just where to put your energy. If you're new to a school, swamped by different opinions, unsure about where to put your energies or simply looking for a fresh start with the right conversations, here's a way to frame up your thinking by eyeing off three things.

1. Eyes on the Teaching and Learning
2. Eyes on the Teams
3. Eyes on Outcomes and Student Wellbeing

These three elements are fundamental to the success of the school. Leaders who intentionally scrutinise these know that they lead directly to better student outcomes in both learning and wellbeing. When school life becomes confusing, complicated and hard to understand, these three elements are one way to bring some perspective back into your thinking and point to the right conversations to be having with people.

Eyes on the Teaching and Learning

Robust conversations about teaching and learning (including adult learning) are always going to engage staff, students and parents. Be careful here as there is a difference between teaching and learning. The best teachers know and use evidence based pedagogy to engage and captivate the learners. These teachers show genuine regard for every learner and they clearly demonstrate a love of the profession. It is not all centred on them. The best teachers see themselves as pedagogical learners too.

Schools where the expectation is that every student will grow in their learning and experience continued success show commitment to the individual student. These schools understand the importance of clearly stating learning intentions and success criteria, they show students what is needed to go from a C grade to a B grade and they continually self-assess their effectiveness to ensure they are focused on the students' learning growth.

As a leader, keeping your eyes firmly on the teaching and learning program is critical to the school's success. The best leaders read widely, have an evidence based opinion which they are not afraid to share, visit classrooms purposefully, know what students are being taught and engage as equals in professional learning.

Here are some sample questions to give a flavour of the types of teaching and learning conversations that matter.

Some questions to consider in understanding teaching and learning

- Do the adults in this school see themselves as learners? What are the examples of adults continually learning themselves? What programs (such as peer-to-peer observation) do we have in place to promote our learning from each other?
- How is job embedded learning conducted in this school?
- Is poor teaching challenged?
- How is our professional learning program tailored to our needs? Who is teaching us?
- Do we talk about the effective pedagogies we implement in our classes?
- Do we all believe that all students can learn at high levels? Do we put limits on what we think students are capable of in their learning?
- What are the conditions for effective learning in our school?
- Are we as good as the literature on learning? Do we know the research on learning and use Action Research effectively?
- How do we clearly state for students the ways they can enhance their learning?
- How does our instruction cater for those students who knew the content / concept before we taught it?
- And those students who 'didn't get it', how do we ensure that they do 'get it'?
- How good can we be? If the students come to this school ready to learn, are we ready to extend and encourage?
- Do our classrooms promote learning? Are they engaging and places that feel safe and look interesting?
- How do we differentiate and individualise our practice for the students?

Eyes on the teams

The second emphasis is about how we take collective responsibility for student success. A school's success comes not from any one individual but from collaborative team work. There's a big gap between cooperation and collaboration in schools. Ezard (2015, p72) believes the highest form of collaboration is where we build collective capacity transforming the work of the team. In collaborative teams clarity of purpose is critical. Flanagan et al. (2016, p86) remind us that without clarity any school improvement strategies often become unsustainable, ineffective and unmanageable.

In any school the basic building block of success will be the strength of the teacher cohort teams (for example the Year 3 teachers with their supporting staff or in a secondary school the Year 10 teachers or perhaps the different faculty teachers gathered). As a leader keep your eyes firmly on these different teams by being involved with their meetings, observing them work, offering practical assistance and where necessary providing a guiding opinion.

Where the members of these teams meet regularly, exchange ideas and approaches, discuss the reasons behind individual student success or otherwise and share their concerns then the school will be on a pathway to success.

Here are some sample questions to give a flavour of the types of collaborative conversations that matter.

Some questions to consider in understanding the strength of the teacher teams

- Are the sentiments behind the school's mission and vision statements evident in the team's conversations ?
- How does the team understand the difference between cooperation and collaboration?
- How do you manage people who put limits on where they'll collaborate?
- What goes on in planning meetings with teachers? Who is present? Are roles defined? Is there clarity of purpose? Are team norms established, visible and observed?
- How do the support specialists (Inclusive Education, pedagogy leaders) interact with the teacher cohorts?
- How involved is the school's leadership team in these teacher cohort planning meetings?
- Is there additional release time provided above the industrial agreement to better enable teachers to collaborate?
- Why is there sometimes resistance to collaboration? Are there particular characteristics of teachers, teaching and school structure that contribute to a tendency to work independently? How could this be changed?
- What can we learn from our colleagues in other cohorts/faculties/schools? How can we be more open to good practice from outside of our school?
- Are you confident the conditions for collaboration are present? (space, time, facility)
- Do we use the benefits of teacher peer-to-peer observation effectively?
- How is feedback to teachers part of the collaborative culture of the school?

Eyes on outcomes and student wellbeing

There is really no point in a contemporary approach to education if it is not driven by better student outcomes. If better outcomes are not being achieved then why move away from rows of desks and all the attention on the teacher at the front of the room? We should be driven by improving the academic and wellbeing outcomes for all students and if that is not occurring then urgently review the situation.

Importantly, all the talk of improved academic outcomes must be balanced by a recognition that student wellbeing is intimately tied up in a student's success. These two are tied together deliberately. To do all this well we must know and respond to the individual, understand and respect the data, constantly search for better ways to engage students in learning, seek new knowledge ourselves and not be afraid to innovate and experiment.

The Australian Curriculum's Personal and Social Capability framework states that: 'Students with well-developed social and emotional skills find it easier to manage themselves, relate to others, develop resilience and a sense of self-worth, resolve conflict, engage in teamwork and feel positive about themselves and the world around them. The development of personal and social capability is a foundation for learning and for citizenship' (Personal and Social Capability (Version 8.4) | The Australian Curriculum (Version 8.4). How will students learn if this basic commitment to wellbeing is not understood?

Leaders need to be constantly eyeing academic progress and student wellbeing. This is the end game really. The wider community will judge a school poorly if either or both of these fall short of expectations. Take your eyes off this and the school will begin to drift.

Here are some sample questions to give a flavour of the types of improved educational outcomes based conversations that matter.

Some questions to consider when focusing on academic and wellbeing improvements

- When students do not progress in their learning what measures are in place to discuss the next steps?
- Are there measurable improvement goals evident about the school?
- Is the emphasis on better student outcomes mentioned in any official school statement?
- How do we triangulate student results to inform our teaching (A-E reporting, NAPLAN results, PAT R and M testing for example)?
- How do we ensure that A-E reporting is well understood by everyone and applied consistently across classes?
- Do we regularly sample students' work, cross mark and discuss with others why particular marks or grades were given?
- When talking about student outcomes do we name the students we are talking about?
- How do we use the data to assist us in better understanding student growth?
- Do we recognise the power of standardised assessment to analyse our effectiveness?
- How do we ensure students are assessment ready?
- How do people respond when the results are poor or below our expectations?
- Are we providing students with a range of assessment experiences?
- How do teachers have input into the summative assessment plan for the school?
- How are formative assessment methods promoted?
- Do students know what is needed from them to move from a C grade to a B grade for example?
- What place do assessment rubrics have in the school?
- What structures are in place to ensure we are aware of individual student wellbeing needs?
- Do we teach students about teamwork, resilience and conflict resolution?
- What knowledge do teachers have of the ACARA Personal and Social Capabilities matrix?
- How are personal and social capabilities incorporated into teachers' curriculum planning?
- Are our crisis management plans tested and amended to ensure the best wrap around occurs when it is needed?

Given the nature of this Episode there are no individual or staff discussion questions listed. There is enough exploratory material above.

 **One step further**

Visit the ACARA Personal and Social Capability learning continuum site to gain a better overview of the place of social and emotional learning in a student's life.

[Personal and Social Capability (Version 8.4) | The Australian Curriculum (Version 8.4)](#)

Personal and social capability encompasses students' personal/emotional and social/relational dispositions, intelligences, sensibilities and learning. It develops effective life skills for students, including understanding and handling themselves, their relationships, learning and work. Although it is named 'Personal and Social capability', the words 'personal/emotional' and 'social/relational' are used interchangeably throughout the literature and within educational organisations. The term 'social and emotional learning' is also often used, as is the SEL acronym.

EPISODE 23

High impact classrooms

TITLE

High impact classrooms

FOCUS

 Individual Leader

 Leadership Team

 School community

WHY READ THIS

There's lots of different classrooms in the school. Many are high impact. The trick is to get more of them.

Me today

What I know about myself as a teacher and like…

What others tell me they see and appreciate in my teaching

My classroom or learning space at its best will…

LOOK LIKE

FEEL LIKE

SOUND LIKE

Underpinned by this school that values, promotes and supports…

And supported by a system that values, promotes and supports…

Me tomorrow

What I know I need to work on…

Who can help me with this learning?

How will I know things are changing for the better?

101

High impact classrooms

High impact classrooms are where all students learn at high levels. These classrooms have a high impact teacher at work.

Here's Fullan:

> The front end task is to hire teachers who have at least four core qualities: (1) high moral commitment relative to the learning of all students regardless of background, (2) strong instructional practice, (3) a desire to work collaboratively, and (4) a commitment to continuous learning (2014, p74).

There is no doubt the teacher that Fullan describes holds the key to student success and that success is greatly compounded when the student has a run of similarly great teachers. High impact classrooms respond positively to the moral challenge in front of all of us: *How do we collectively and individually make a lasting positive difference to the lives of students in classrooms?*

Many of the Episodes in this publication are about leadership. This Episode is about leadership in the classroom. And leadership is needed because we can become lost in the social and cultural battles going on around education and lose sight of this moral challenge quite easily. High impact teachers keep their singular focus.

These days the threat of industrial action is commonplace, bureaucracy seems restrictive and people are worn down by a steady stream of media criticism and unfavourable political commentary about more perceived NAPLAN failures. Student behaviour issues and gender identity debates mean that for many, schools are nothing like they used to be. Critics and experts abound. Little wonder the average person is left confused.

So what sets high impact teachers apart? What are they doing differently that responds to the moral challenge that every teacher faces?

An often overlooked factor is that high impact teachers use the prescribed curriculum effectively. They do not rely on old units of work, subscription based web services, textbooks or computer-generated programs of one sort or another. High impact teachers know the curriculum because they have read the curriculum and they talk to colleagues about the curriculum. Understanding the various components of these key documents and how the parts connect to form the body of knowledge and skills needed for the students is critical.

This Episode is about teachers and their classrooms and asks 'how do you move from a classroom to a high impact classroom?' In more philosophical terms, what has to happen to ensure the moral challenge is met?

Putting the classroom at the centre

The starting point for a high impact classroom is the teacher in question. The learning space follows because it is deliberately shaped by that teacher and is in turn supported by a school and then a system environment that promotes certain values and expectations. One important expectation is that all teachers collaborate. This is the ecosystem in which the school exists.

In whatever shape they appear, classrooms or learning spaces are at the centre of the school. A high impact classroom in this publication is not defined by any particular shape, architectural style, furniture or fittings. A high impact classroom can indeed be a single classroom or open plan, team teaching space or in a highrise building. A high impact classroom is not defined by any single well regarded and passionately held educational philosophy of which there are many (such as Montersori, various inquiry models or the Baccalaureate approach as examples).

High impact classrooms look the same as any other learning space from the outside. There's at least one teacher, other adults are in sight and there are walls and doors and other classrooms close by.

And yet, if we are honest, we can know the difference shortly after entering because not all classrooms are equal. There is a different atmosphere in a high impact classroom. The movement and presence of the teacher tells the story, the walls tell the story, the student engagement level tells the story, the interesting elements in the room also tell the story. The quality of all the student work is obvious. The indications are that something exciting is going on here.

> Effective teachers have a profound influence on student learning. The difference two effective teachers in a row makes is amazing.

High impact teachers exert their considerable influence in subtle ways. Their classroom does the talking and is notable for the number of people who come and go, exchanging ideas, practice and information.

We start with the qualities of the teacher, move to the learning space the teacher creates and then focus on the school itself and finally, the system that supports the school.

A high impact teacher is someone who:

- Loves teaching and respects all students
- Has a strong moral purpose and believes all students can learn at high levels
- Has a growth mindset, is reflective and can change course if necessary
- Knows the curriculum and can converse easily with others about the curriculum
- Is organised, planned and ready for the day, week and term ahead
- Holds high expectations of themselves and of the students
- Knows every learner and knows how to challenge every learner
- Communicates regularly with parents and treats parents with respect
- Uses the available school and system support effectively
- Implements positive behaviour for learning strategies
- Understands data and uses data wisely to ensure learning gaps are addressed
- Seeks student and colleague feedback
- Promotes and participates in collaboration and never professes to know everything
- Is an effective 'influencer', someone who quietly promotes these best practices.

A high impact classroom is a learning space that:

- Is engaging on entry with the third teacher (use of physical space) evident
- Is flexible and contemporary allowing for different design and use of spaces
- Offers the students high challenge with high support
- Proudly displays current student work and promotes quality work
- Provides examples of quality work for students to model off
- Displays teacher created work, anchor charts, resources and reference material
- Has a welcoming, calm feel where the high level of student engagement is evident.

Teachers and classrooms are underpinned by a high impact school environment that:

- Promotes collaboration, professional learning, team and consistent pedagogy
- Has clear norms and practices and holds people to account
- Promotes a safe work environment that encourages dialogue
- Has systems to ensure compliance is well managed and not burdensome to teachers
- Has solid meeting and engagement routines that are focused on learning and wellbeing
- Is well documented so everyone understands the intentions and expectations
- Has a leadership team that is visible, invested in the staff, the learners and is responsive to changing circumstances
- Values all support staff and promotes their learning
- Includes parents as first order partners.

And schools are supported by a high impact system that:

- Reminds people why the schools exist
- Adopts a 'not too tight, not too loose' philosophy that promotes creativity and still supports consistency
- Has a consistent message, values clarity and precision in language
- Collects and uses data transparently, effectively and ethically
- Is focused on learning growth, building capacity and school improvement
- Targets professional learning and delivers quality learning in mixed formats
- Values the people and promotes excellence
- Supports teachers with diverse learner needs
- Has systems to ensure compliance is well managed and not burdensome.

Individual reflection

- How do you see the moral challenges facing education today affecting your classroom?
- How can you sharpen your own classroom practices to better reflect a high impact environment?

Staff discussion

- What are some practical measures to lift school performance to another level?
- How can we use the system resources available to us more effectively?

One step further

Can you answer the question: What workplace norms have you disrupted this year? In the school is there one current workplace norm or practice that is limiting the growth of teachers and what can be done about this practice? If teachers have a moral challenge, so too does the leadership. Some practices are not conducive to making a lasting and positive difference to the lives of teachers (no different to the students).

EPISODE 24

TITLE

The observed culture

FOCUS

 Individual Leader

 Leadership Team

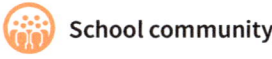 School community

WHY READ THIS

What are you seeing and how often do you see it?

The learning culture

1. **Never seen**: means never seen
2. **Practised occasionally**: means some staff, occasionally
3. **Practised frequently**: means most of the staff, most of the time
4. **Embedded**: means all staff, all the time

Teachers in our school…	Please indicate rating (✔) 1	2	3	4	Evidence for this rating
Contribute equally					
Discuss student results reflecting on the impact of our teaching					
Give freely of their individual skill or special interest					
Freely share teaching strategies with each other (successful or otherwise)					
Observe colleagues teaching and discuss what was observed with them					
Talk about teaching and learning challenges in positive ways					
Are able to resolve any hurt or misunderstanding effectively					
Have the syllabus/curriculum open when meeting and refer to it when planning					
Adopt a common assessment schedule					
Are committed to the school's vision and mission					
Use all available people resource (learning support, pedagogy leaders, Principal, AP, etc)					
Own the results of all students					
Are comfortable when it does not go right the first time					
Can be open and say that they are unsure about how to teach a topic					
Discuss the notion of High Expectations					
Work together to ensure Consistent Teacher Judgement (consistent A-E standards)					
Use data to understand the effect of our teaching					
Talk more about learning than behaviour					

The learning culture

If you're new to a school as an employee, people paint a picture of the school in different ways. The best way to understand what's really going on is to observe it in action.

The graphic for this Episode provides a number of cultural markers that together indicate something of the overall learning culture in the school. If these indicators are practised frequently or indeed are embedded in the life of the school, then this says much about the positive learning culture to be found here.

Everyone, even the new employee plays a role in shaping the culture of a school. Culture is never solely a leadership team responsibility.

Culture is easily understood as the 'way things are done around here' and with more depth as, (i) the systems that are in place to get things done, (ii) the symbols about the school that represent who we are and what we stand for and most importantly (iii) the behaviours expected and observed in the school.

Positive cultures

One culture you definitely want is an enriching, positive culture. In schools with a positive culture there is a strong focus on building people and not so much on building physical structures. Teachers and leadership teams see themselves as learners, as people who have far more strength as a collective rather than as individual teachers who might cooperate (when it suits). There is a clear focus on learning and a belief that all students can grow and make progress. To achieve this there are agreed frameworks and philosophies (like Fullan's Coherence Framework, 2016) and collaborative planning. Central to success is high expectations for all students and themselves.

The desire to move to a professionally satisfying culture is an admirable goal. These days there's more support for schools to achieve this goal. Progressive system administrations adopt a strong focus on developing teacher skills in pedagogy and student management and offer workshops on diversity, inclusion and wellbeing. Staffing schedules are enhanced with specialist pedagogical support for teachers. Culture is a hot topic.

Understanding of the notion of learning in positive cultures

There are many pointers to the understanding of the notion of learning in the school's culture. In days past the teacher was always right, possessed the knowledge, did not need to consult and delivered accordingly. In contemporary education there is an almost total about face. A relational, collaborative approach to learning means everyone is a learner and should be open to new ways, to being observed and challenged. Dialogue, questioning and trust is central.

Learning for everyone is supported in these positive cultures through the provision of additional release time to collaborate with colleagues. This collaboration is highly valued. Support staff like literacy and pedagogical coaches are routinely in classrooms working alongside teachers. There is an understanding of the place of data collection and data analysis so that every child's learning needs is well understood and targeted.

The principal and leadership team are indistinguishable as learners themselves. They show this by being in classrooms, by attending professional learning with the teachers, by asking questions and following up on requested support. They do not adopt the expert model and admit to not knowing if they don't know.

> Am I able to set aside old notions, thoughts and prejudices and enter into a growth mindset that demonstrates a willingness to collaborate with others?

The Victorian Education Department focuses on 10 principles that bring together the best available research on school improvement. These are all learning culture markers.

- **Student learning focus:** School improvement starts with an unwavering focus on student learning.
- **Collective responsibility:** For every child to achieve, every adult must take responsibility for their learning.
- **Instructional leadership:** Effective school leaders focus on teaching and learning.
- **Collective efficacy:** Teachers make better instructional decisions together.
- **Adult learning:** Teachers learn best with others, on the job.
- **Privileged time:** Effective schools provide time and forums for teacher conversations about student learning.
- **Continuous improvement:** Effective teams improve through recurring cycles of diagnosing student learning needs, and planning, implementing and evaluating teaching responses to them.
- **Evidence driven:** Effective professional learning and practice are evidence-based and data-driven.
- **System focus:** The most effective school leaders contribute to the success of other schools.
- **Integrated regional support:** Schools in improving systems are supported by teams of experts who know the communities they work in.

Professional learning communities (education.vic.gov.au)

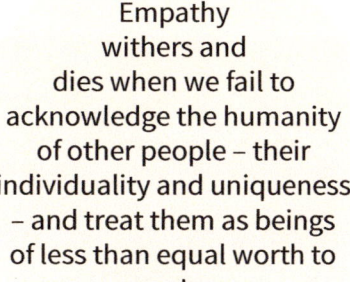

Empathy withers and dies when we fail to acknowledge the humanity of other people – their individuality and uniqueness – and treat them as beings of less than equal worth to ourselves.

Krznaric (2014)

Individual reflection

- In what ways am I actively shaping the learning culture of the school?
- If I am completely honest, are all these ways contributing to a positive culture or on reflection can I act in slightly different ways to bring a more positive me to the interaction?
- When do I know that I am not open to new ideas?

Staff discussion

- (From the graphic) What do we have to collectively do to move a Rating 2 to a Rating 3 in any question listed?
- Are there changes to structures that will further improve the culture by allowing more time to collaborate?
- How might a peer-to-peer observation process improve collaboration?

One step further

If you're reading this as a principal would you consider:

- Creating 'in school' teacher collaboration time to allow for school funded additional time over system provided time? WHY NOT?
- Raise the topic of a Professional Learning Community with the Leadership Team? WHY NOT?
- Ask to visit a school with a Professional Learning Community structure in place? WHY NOT?
- Ask a colleague principal to take the journey together on a Learning Community path with you? WHY NOT?

References

Anderson, M., Cawsey, C. (2008). Learning for Leadership: Building a school of professional practice. ACER, Melbourne.

Australian Council for Educational Research (ACER), Commonwealth Department of Education, Employment and Workplace Relations (2012), National School Improvement Tool. Canberra.

Australian Government, Commonwealth Ombudsman Office, Better Practice Complaint Handling Guide, https://www.ombudsman.gov.au/__data/assets/pdf_file/0019/112276/Better-Practice-Guide-FINAL-v6-A2111312.pdf

Australian Institute for Teaching and School Leadership. (2012). Australian Teacher Performance and Development Framework (aitsl.edu.au)

Australian Institute for Teaching and School Leadership. (2017). Australian Professional Standards for Teachers. www.aitsl.edu.au/

Barber, M. & Mourshead, M. (2007). How the world's best performing school systems come out on top, McKinsey and Company, New York, accessed at https://www.mckinsey.com/industries/education/our-insights/how-the-worlds-best-performing-school-systems-come-out-on-top.

Bergsagel, V. (2007). Architecture for Achievement: Building patterns for small school learning, Eagle Chatter Press, Mercer Island, WA.

Bezzina, M. (2018). Authentic Learning: Why it matters and what we can do about it, Sydney Catholic Schools, Leichhardt, Sydney.

Bradberry, T., Greaves, J. (2009), Emotional Intelligence 2.0. TalentSmart Publishing.

Brooks, A., Edwards, K. (2014). Consulting in Uncertainty: The power of inquiry. Routledge.

Browning, P. (2015). Compelling Leadership: The importance of trust and how to get it (ibook). Centre for Research, Innovation and Future Development, Compelling Leadership Book – Compelling Leadership.

Bryk, A.S., Gomez. L.M., Grunow, A., & LeMahieu, P.G. (2015). Learning to Improve: How America's schools can get better at getting better, Harvard Education Press, Cambridge, M.A.

Carrington, N. (undated material sourced from a digital presentation by the author) www.griffith.edu.au

Centre for Education Statistics and Evaluation (2020), What Works Best: 2020 update, NSW Department of Education, cese.nsw.gov.au.

Covey, Stephen. M.R. (2008). The Speed of Trust, The one thing that changes everything. Free Press, New York.

Cox, D. (2023). Why everyday stress could be the key to a healthy old age, The Observer Newspaper, January 01.

Danielson, C. (2016). Talk about Teaching: Leading professional conversations. Sage Publications.

Davey, L. (2023). Aim to Create Accountability via Compassion. Harvard Business Review, distributed by NYT Syndicate, cited in The Weekend Australian Newspaper, March 04 05, 2023, p48.

DuFour, R. (2004). What is a "Professional Learning Community"? Educational Leadership, 61(8), p6.

DuFour, R., DuFour, R., Eaker, R., Many, T., Mattos, M. (2016). Learning by Doing, A handbook for professional learning communities at work. Hawker Brownlow Education, Melbourne.

DuFour, R., Marzano, R. (2011). Leaders of Learning, Hawker Brownlow Education, Melbourne, Victoria.

Dweck, C. (2012). Mindset: How you can fulfill your potential, Robinson, London. As sighted in Ritchhart, R., (2015). Creating Cultures of Thinking, p57.

Ezard, T. (2015). The Buzz: Creating a thriving and collaborative learning culture. Self published, PO Box 21130, Little Lonsdale St., Melbourne.

Ezard, T. (2017). Glue: The stuff that binds us together. Self published, PO Box 21130, Little Lonsdale St., Melbourne.

Ezard, T. (2021), Ferocious Warmth: School leaders who inspire and transform. Self published, PO Box 21130, Little Lonsdale St., Melbourne.

Flanagan, T., Grift, G., Lipscombe, K., Sloper, C., Wills, J. (2016). Transformative Collaboration, Five commitments for leading a professional learning community. Hawker Brownlow, Melbourne.

Fisk, S. (2021). Leading Data Informed Change in Schools. Solution Tree, Melbourne.

Fullan, M. (2010). The Moral Imperative Realised, Corwin: Sage Publications Inc, Thousand Oaks, California.

Fullan, M. (2014). The Principal: Three keys to maximising impact. Jossey Bass.

Fullan, M., Quinn, J. (2016). Coherence: The right drivers in action for schools, districts and systems. Corwin: Sage Publications Inc, Thousand Oaks, California..

Hargreaves, A. & Fullan, M. (2012). Professional Capital: Transforming teaching in every school. Teachers College Press, USA.

Hargreaves, A., O'Connor, M. T. (2018). Collaborative Professionalism: When teaching together means learning for all. Corwin, CA.

Hargreaves, A. (2000). Teachers and Teaching: history and practice, Vol 6, No 2, Journal Carfax Publishing, Oxfordshire, p6.

Hargreaves, A. (n.d.) AZQuotes.com, retrieved 03/10/19, from AZQuotes.com, website: https://www.azquotes.com/quote/817140.

Hargreaves, A., Fullan, M. (2012). Professional Capital: Being professional and being a professional - Transforming teachers in every school, Teachers' College Press.

Hannah, S. & and Avolio, T. (2010). Moral Potency: Building the capacity for character-based leadership, Consulting Psychology Journal: Practice and research, 62(4) p10.

Harris, A., Jones, M., Huffman J. (2018). Teachers Leading Educational Reform: The Power of Professional Learning Communities. Routledge, New York.

Harris, A., & Jones, M. (2010) Professional learning communities and system improvement. Improving Schools, 13(2), p172-181.

Hattie, J. in (2016), Sharratt, L., & Planche, B., Leading Collaborative Learning, Corwin Press, California.

Hattie, J. (2009). Visible Learning: A synthesis of over 800 meta-analyses relating to student achievement, Hawker Brownlow Education, Melbourne, Victoria.

Harvey, W. (1649) Exercitationes Duae Anatomicae de Circulatione Sanguinis, ad Joannem Riolanem, Filium, Parisiensem (Two Anatomical Exercises on the Circulation of the Blood).

Hipp, K. & Huffman, J. (2010). Demystifying professional learning communities: School leadership at its best. Lanham, MD: Rowman & Littlefield Education.

Ingvarson, L. (2016). How Strong is Your School as a Professional Community? Australian Council for Educational Research, Melbourne. How strong is your school as a professional community? (slideshare.net)

Ingvarson, L. (2018) Learning Community Framework, Australian Council for Educational Research, online resource from www.acer.edu.au/school-improvement-services/professional-community-framework.

Jefferson, M., Anderson, M. (2017). Transforming Schools: Creativity, critical reflection, communication, collaboration. Bloomsbury, New York.

Kirtman, L. (2013). Leadership and Teams: The missing piece of the educational reform puzzle. Pearson Education.

Kotter, J. (2012) Leading Change. Harvard Business Review Press, United States.

Knight, J. (2016.) Better Conversations: Coaching ourselves and each other to be more credible, caring and connected. Corwin, California.

Knight, J., Knight, J.R., Carlson, C. (2015). The Reflection Guide for Better Conversations: Coaching ourselves and each other to be more credible, caring and connected. Corwin Press, California.

Krznaric, R. (2014) in, Knight, J. (2016.) Better Conversations: Coaching ourselves and each other to be more credible, caring and connected, p43. Corwin, California.

Leithwood, K., Day, C., Sammons, P., Harris, A., & Hopkins, D. (2006). Seven strong claims about successful school leadership. England: NCSL.

Louis, K. S. & Marks, H. M. (1998). Does the professional community affect the classroom? Teachers' work and student experiences in restructuring schools. American Journal of Education, p532-575.

Ludema, J.D., Wilmot, T.B. & Srivastva, S. (1997). Organisational hope: Reaffirming the constructive task of social and organisational inquiry. Human Relations, Volume 50, Issue 8, August, pp 1015–1052.

Martinez, S., Stager, G. (2019). Invent to Learn: Tinkering and engineering in the classroom. Constructing Modern Knowledge Press.

Marzano, R.J. (2003). What Works in Schools: Translating research into action, Hawker Brownlow Education, Melbourne, Victoria.

New South Wales Department of Education, What Works Best: 2020 Update. Centre for Education Statistics and Evaluation, What works best 2020 update (nsw.gov.au)

Newton, J.F.(1880-1950). Top 25 Quotes by Joseph Fort Newton, A=Z Quotes (azquotes.com)

Nichols, T., (2019). The Death of Expertise: The campaign against established knowledge and why it matters, Oxford University Press, N.Y.

Parker, A., (2012). The Negotiators ToolKit: A practical guide to success in the home, office, factory, farm and boardroom. Peak Performance Development, www.peakpd.com

Patterson et al. (2008). Influencer: The power to change anything. McGraw-Hill Education (India) Pvt Limited, cited in DuFour et al. (2016). Learning by Doing: A handbook for professional learning communities at work.

Pearlin, L. (1989). The Sociological Study of Stress. The Journal of Health and Social Behaviour, 30: 241-256.

Pink, D. (2009). Drive: The surprising truth about what motivates us. Canongate Paperback, New York.

Ritchhart, R. (2015). Creating Cultures of Thinking: The 8 forces we must master to truly transform our schools. Jossey Bass, San Francisco.

Robinson, V. (2018). Reduce change to increase improvement, Corwin, California.

Robinson V., & Timperley, H. (2007). The Leadership of the Improvement of Teaching and Learning: Lessons from initiatives with positive outcomes for students, Australian Journal of Education, 51(3), p635-674.

Robinson, V., Lloyd, C., & Rowe, K. (2008). The impact of leadership on student outcomes: An analysis of the differential effects of leadership type, Educational Administration Quarterly, 44(5) p635-674.

Robinson, V., Hohepa, M., Lloyd, C. (2009). School Leadership and Student Outcomes: Identifying what works and why, Best evidence Synthesis. Crown, Auckland.

Robinson, V., Le Fevre, D., Sinnema, C. (2016). Open to Learning Leadership: How to build trust while tackling tough issues. Hawker Brownlow Education, Melbourne.

Rosenholtz, S. (1989). Teachers' Workplace, Longman Press, N.Y.

Senge, P., (1990). The Fifth Discipline: The Art and Practice of the Learning Organisation, from Knight, J. (2016) Better Conversations: Coaching ourselves and each other to be more credible, caring and connected. Corwin, California.

Sharratt, L., Planche, B. (2016). Leading Collaborative Learning: Empowering excellence. Sage Publications.

State of Victoria, Department of Education and Training, (2017). High Impact Teaching Strategies (HITS): Excellent in teaching and learning. Melbourne.

Timperley, H., Wilson, A., Barrar, H. & Fung, I. (2007). Teacher professional learning and development: Best evidence synthesis. University of Auckland. Auckland, New Zealand

Timperley, H., Ell, F., Le Fevre, D., Twyford, K. (2020). Leading Professional Learning: Practical strategies for impact in schools. ACER, Melbourne.

Turner, J., Stets, J. (2005). The Sociology of Emotions. Cambridge University Press, New York.

University of Missouri Inclusion, Diversity and Equity Department, Guide to Facilitating Dialogues, facilitating-dialogue.pdf (missouri.edu)

Vescio, V., Ross, D. & Adams, A. (2008). A review of research on the impact of professional learning communities on teaching practice and student learning. Teaching and Teacher Education, University of Florida, Gainesville, 24(1), p80-91

Walker, W. (2015). Leadership in a Digital Age, Oration, October 02, ACEL publication, Sydney.

Whittaker, T. (2010). Leading School Change: 9 Strategies to Bring Everybody on Board, 2013, Routledge UK.

Williams, K., Hierck, T. (2015). Starting a Movement, Building culture from the inside out in professional learning communities. Solution Tree, Sydney.

Notes

www.ingramcontent.com/pod-product-compliance
Lightning Source LLC
Chambersburg PA
CBHW050853010526
44107CB00047BA/1602